SLIM AND HEALTHY COOKING

GOOD HOUSEKEEPING
STEP-BY-STEP COOKERY

SLIM AND HEALTHY COOKING

Guild Publishing/Ebury Press
LONDON

Consultant editor: Jeni Wright
Editor: Barbara Croxford
Design by Mike Leaman
Drawings by John Woodcock and Kate Simunek
Photographs by Peter Myers

Cover photograph: Minted Lamb Meatballs (page 65), Melon and Prawn Salad (page 33)

Filmset by Advanced Filmsetters (Glasgow) Ltd

Printed and bound in Italy by
New Interlitho, S.p.a., Milan

CONTENTS

COOKERY NOTES

Follow either metric or imperial measures for the recipes in this book as they are not inter-changeable. Sets of spoon measures are available in both metric and imperial size to give accurate measurement of small quantities. All spoon measures are level unless otherwise stated. When measuring milk we have used the exact conversion of 568 ml (1 pint).

* Size 4 eggs should be used except when otherwise stated.
● Calories for recipes are calculated using whole milk.

OVEN TEMPERATURE CHART

°C	°F	Gas mark
110	225	$\frac{1}{4}$
130	250	$\frac{1}{2}$
140	275	1
150	300	2
170	325	3
180	350	4
190	375	5
200	400	6
220	425	7
230	450	8
240	475	9

METRIC CONVERSION SCALE

LIQUID				SOLID		
Imperial	*Exact conversion*	*Recommended ml*		*Imperial*	*Exact conversion*	*Recommended g*
$\frac{1}{4}$ pint	142 ml	150 ml		1 oz	28.35 g	25 g
$\frac{1}{2}$ pint	284 ml	300 ml		2 oz	56.7 g	50 g
1 pint	568 ml	600 ml		4 oz	113.4 g	100 g
$1\frac{1}{2}$ pints	851 ml	900 ml		8 oz	226.8 g	225 g
$1\frac{3}{4}$ pints	992 ml	1 litre		12 oz	340.2 g	350 g
For quantities of $1\frac{3}{4}$ pints and over,				14 oz	397.0 g	400 g
litres and fractions of a litre have				16 oz (1 lb)	453.6 g	450 g
been used.				1 kilogram (kg) equals 2.2 lb.		

KEY TO SYMBOLS

$\boxed{1.00*}$ Indicates minimum preparation and cooking times in hours and minutes. They do not include prepared items in the list of ingredients; calcu-lated times apply only to the method. An asterisk * indicates extra time should be allowed, so check the note below symbols.

⌂ Chef's hats indicate degree of difficulty of a recipe: no hat means it is straightforward; one hat slightly more complicated; two hats indicates that it is for more advanced cooks.

£ Indicates a recipe which is good value for money; £ £ indicates an expensive recipe. No £ sign indicates an inexpensive recipe.

✳ Indicates that a recipe will freeze. If there is no symbol, the recipe is unsuitable for freezing. An asterisk * indicates special freezer instructions so check the note immediately below the symbols.

$\boxed{309\ cals}$ Indicates calories per serving, including any sugges-tions (e.g. cream, to serve) given in the ingredients.

SLIM AND HEALTHY COOKING

This is not a cranky 'health food' book. It is a cookbook about healthy eating, about choosing and using the best ingredients to keep you and your family as healthy, slim and fit as possible—without indulging in faddy diets. Food plays a vital part in determining our health, and much is talked about the importance of a well-balanced diet, low in fat and high in fibre. This recipe book sets out to bring you interesting dishes which illustrate this point. To be healthy and slim doesn't necessarily mean a complete change of eating habits, but perhaps a new awareness of which foods are best eaten regularly, and which are best left alone or only eaten in moderation. In this book the accent is on fresh natural ingredients, avoiding the use of commercial convenience and pre-packaged foods, artificial flavourings, preservatives and additives. Wherever possible, ingredients are low-fat and high-fibre. Although not specified in the ingredients lists of individual recipes, you will probably choose to use skimmed or semi-skimmed milk, and low-fat vegetable margarines, which are preferable to high-cholesterol butter and other animal fats. Raw brown sugar and wholemeal flour are generally specified throughout the book, but if you find a mixture of half wholemeal and half white flour gives better baking results, then by all means use whatever suits you best. Calorie counts are given for all recipes in the colour section.

There are many vegetarian dishes in the book, plus a special Vegetarian Main Course chapter. Dishes for vegans (those who eat neither meat, fish, fowl nor dairy produce and eggs) are not included, as the vegan diet is a specialised subject which cannot be covered adequately in a conventional cookbook of this kind.

Breakfasts

Get the day off to a good start with a nutritious breakfast using wholefood ingredients. Fried breakfasts should be a thing of the past if you're thinking healthy and slim. Cereals, grains, fresh and dried fruits, nuts, yogurt and vegetable vitality drinks are far more healthy in the morning. They will give you the necessary fibre for a healthy diet — and sustain you better through long, busy days.

SMOKED FISH KEDGEREE

$\boxed{0.55}$ £ $\boxed{276 \text{ cals}}$

Serves 4

175 g (6 oz) long grain brown rice
salt and freshly ground pepper
275 g (10 oz) smoked haddock
25 g (1 oz) margarine or butter
1 hard-boiled egg, chopped
30 ml (2 tbsp) chopped fresh
    parsley
juice of $\frac{1}{2}$ lemon

1 Place the rice in a large sauce-pan of boiling salted water and cook for about 35 minutes or according to packet instructions until tender.

2 Meanwhile, place the haddock in a pan, cover with water and poach for about 15 minutes.

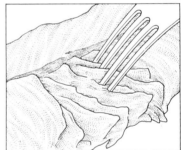

3 Drain the fish well, then flake the fish, discarding the skin and bones.

4 Drain the rice well. Melt the margarine in a frying pan, add the rice, haddock, egg and parsley and stir over moderate heat for a few minutes until warmed through. Add the lemon juice and seasoning to taste, turn into a warmed serving dish and serve immediately.

MUESLI

$\boxed{0.10}$ £ $\boxed{175 \text{ cals}}$

Makes 14 servings

250 g (9 oz) porridge oats

75 g (3 oz) wholewheat flakes

50 g (2 oz) bran buds

75 g (3 oz) sunflower seeds

175 g (6 oz) sultanas

175 g (6 oz) dried pears (or apricots, figs or peaches), cut into small pieces

1 Mix together the porridge oats, wholewheat flakes, bran buds, sunflower seeds, sultanas and dried pears. (The dried fruits can be varied according to taste and availability, but keep the ratio of grains to fruit about the same.)

2 The dry muesli will keep fresh for several weeks if stored in an airtight container.

MUESLI

The original idea for muesli as a breakfast dish came from a Swiss doctor called Max Bircher-Benner, which is why some brands of muesli are called 'Bircher Muesli'. Dr Bircher-Benner had a clinic in Zurich at the beginning of the century, where he prescribed muesli for his patients, to be eaten both at breakfast time and supper. The original muesli was based on fresh fruit, with porridge oats (the German word *muesli* means gruel) added. This is why muesli cereal is usually eaten with fruit—in this recipe dried fruit is suggested, but fresh fruit may be used instead.

DRIED FRUIT COMPOTE

0.15* £ 80 cals

* plus overnight macerating

Serves 6

50 g (2 oz) dried apple rings

50 g (2 oz) dried apricots

50 g (2 oz) dried figs

300 ml ($\frac{1}{2}$ pint) unsweetened orange juice

300 ml ($\frac{1}{2}$ pint) water

25 g (1 oz) hazelnuts

1 Cut the dried apples, apricots and figs into chunky pieces and place in a bowl.

2 Mix together the unsweetened orange juice and water and pour over the fruit in the bowl. Cover and leave to macerate in the refrigerator overnight.

3 The next day, spread the hazelnuts out in a grill pan and toast under a low to moderate heat, shaking the pan frequently until the hazelnuts are browned evenly on all sides.

4 Tip the hazelnuts into a clean tea-towel and rub them while they are still hot to remove the skins.

5 Chop the hazelnuts roughly using an automatic chopper or large cook's knife. Sprinkle over the compote just before serving.

APPLE AND DATE PORRIDGE

| 0.20 | £ | 216 cals |

Serves 6

100 g (4 oz) dried dates

1 large cooking apple

25 g (1 oz) margarine or butter

25 g (1 oz) bran

15 ml (1 tbsp) dark soft brown sugar

1.1 litres (2 pints) water

175 g (6 oz) porridge oats

1 Stone and roughly chop the dried dates. Roughly chop (but do not peel) a large cooking apple, discarding the core.

2 Melt the margarine in a large saucepan, stir in the bran and brown sugar and cook, stirring, for about 2 minutes.

3 Pour the water into the pan, then sprinkle in the porridge oats. Bring the mixture to the boil, stirring.

4 Add the dates and apple, and simmer, stirring, for about 5 minutes or until of the desired consistency. Serve hot.

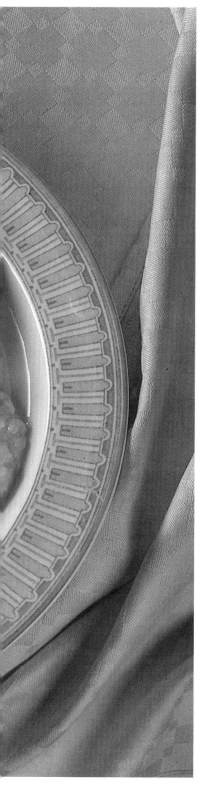

BRAN MUFFINS

| 0.45 | ✳ | 420 cals |

Serves 4

50 g (2 oz) muscovado sugar

50 g (2 oz) margarine or butter

30 ml (2 tbsp) honey

175 g (6 oz) self-raising wholewheat flour

50 g (2 oz) bran

1.25 ml (¼ tsp) salt

1 egg, beaten

150 ml (¼ pint) natural yogurt

60 ml (4 tbsp) milk

1 Gently melt the sugar, margarine and honey together in a heavy-based pan. Remove from the heat.

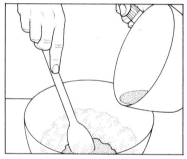

2 Mix the flour, bran and salt together in a bowl. Make a well in the centre and pour in the melted mixture. Stir well to mix, then add the egg, yogurt and milk. Beat to a smooth batter.

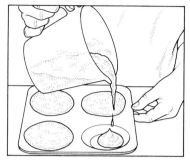

3 Divide the batter equally between 4 well-greased Yorkshire pudding tins. Bake in the oven at 190°C (375°F) mark 5 for 25 minutes until well risen. Turn out on to a wire rack and cool for 5 minutes before serving.

Menu Suggestion

Serve the muffins warm for breakfast, split in half and buttered. Top with fluffy scrambled eggs, or spread with honey or a reduced sugar jam or marmalade.

BRAN MUFFINS

To make scrambled eggs to serve with muffins, lightly whisk together 4 eggs, 60 ml (4 tablespoons) milk and seasoning to taste. Melt 40 g (1½ oz) butter or margarine in a heavy-based saucepan, pour in the egg and milk mixture and cook over gentle heat, stirring constantly with a wooden spoon. Cook just for a few minutes until the mixture thickens and looks creamy, then immediately remove from the heat and pile on top of the muffins. Take great care when scrambling eggs that you do not overcook the mixture. Do not leave it in the pan for more than a second or two before serving—even the heat of the pan can make the eggs rubbery.

VEGETABLE VITALITY DRINK

0.40* | 293 cals

* including 30 minutes infusing

Serves 1

50 g (2 oz) shredded coconut
300 ml ($\frac{1}{2}$ pint) boiling water
225 g (8 oz) carrots
juice of $\frac{1}{2}$ lemon
5 ml (1 tsp) wheatgerm oil

1 Put the coconut in a heatproof jug, pour on the boiling water and stir well to mix. Leave to infuse for 30 minutes.

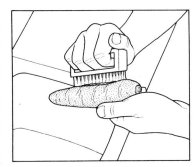

2 Meanwhile, scrub the carrots with a stiff vegetable brush to remove any soil from their skins. Grate into a blender or food processor, add the lemon juice and blend until the carrots are broken down to a pulp.

3 Strain the carrot pulp through a sieve into a jug, then strain in the milk from the coconut. Add the wheatgerm oil and whisk vigorously to combine. Pour into a long glass and serve immediately.

YOGURT VITALITY DRINK

0.05 | 280 cals

Serves 1

1 small banana
10 ml (2 tsp) wheatgerm
juice of 1 orange
150 ml ($\frac{1}{4}$ pint) natural yogurt
1 egg yolk

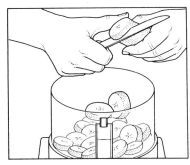

1 Peel the banana and slice straight into a blender or food processor.

2 Add the wheatgerm, orange juice, yogurt and egg yolk and blend to a smooth mixture. Pour into a long glass and serve immediately.

FRUITY VITALITY DRINK

0.05 | 195 cals

Serves 1

2 pink grapefruit
1 lemon
1 egg
10 ml (2 tsp) honey, or to taste
5 ml (1 tsp) wheatgerm

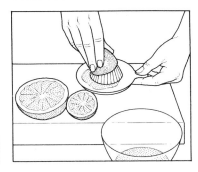

1 Squeeze the juice from the grapefruit and lemon, and pour into a blender or food processor.

2 Add the egg, honey and wheatgerm and blend until well combined. Taste for sweetness and add more honey if liked. Pour into a long glass and serve immediately.

Soups and Starters

In a 'healthy and slim' diet, soups and starters should be light and refreshing, full of freshness and flavour — to set the mood for the rest of the meal. Portions should be quite small, and attention to detail and presentation more important than actual quantity. Don't forget that these recipes also make nutritious snacks or light meals in themselves—they don't have to be served as a first course of a meal.

ICED SWEET PEPPER SOUP

0.35* £ 48 cals

* plus 30 minutes cooling and 2 hours chilling

Serves 4

60 ml (4 tbsp) chopped fresh coriander

225 g (8 oz) sweet red peppers

125 g (4 oz) onion

225 g (8 oz) ripe tomatoes

900 ml (1½ pints) vegetable or chicken stock

150 ml (¼ pint) milk

salt and freshly ground pepper

1 Make the coriander ice cubes. Put the chopped coriander into an ice-cube tray, top up with water and freeze.

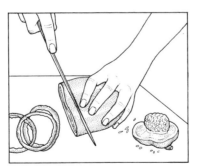

2 Wipe the peppers. Cut the stem end off, scoop out the seeds and slice the flesh. Skin and slice the onion, and slice the tomatoes.

3 Place the peppers in a large saucepan with the onion, tomatoes and stock. Bring to the boil, then lower the heat, cover and simmer for about 15 minutes or until the vegetables are tender. Drain, reserving the liquid.

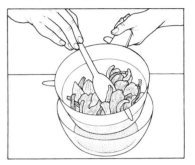

4 Sieve the vegetables, or purée them in a blender or food processor, then sieve the purée to remove the tomato seeds.

5 Combine the reserved liquid, vegetable purée and milk in a bowl with seasoning to taste. Cool for 30 minutes, then chill in the refrigerator for at least 2 hours before serving. Serve with coriander ice cubes.

Menu Suggestion

Serve as a refreshing start to a summer meal.

ICED SWEET PEPPER SOUP

Do not confuse the herb coriander with the spice of the same name. In this recipe, the fresh herb is used. Looking rather like frondy parsley, it is available at many supermarkets and also at continental and oriental specialist shops. Its flavour is highly aromatic, much stronger than parsley. The spice coriander is used extensively in Indian cookery; it is available as whole seeds and in ground form. The herb and the spice are not interchangeable in recipes, so take care which one you use.

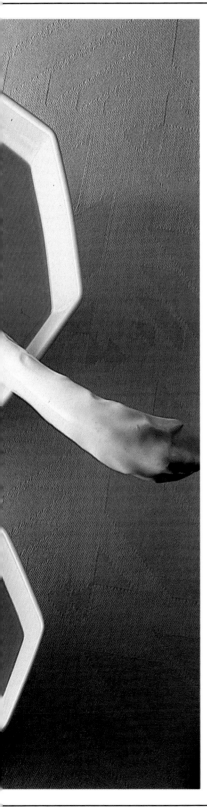

VEGETABLE SOUP

| 1.00 | £ | 281 cals |

Serves 4

350 g (12 oz) carrot

225 g (8 oz) turnip

175 g (6 oz) onion

225 g (8 oz) celery

5 ml (1 tsp) chopped fresh thyme
   or 2.5 ml ($\frac{1}{2}$ tsp) dried

5 ml (1 tsp) chopped fresh basil or
   2.5 ml ($\frac{1}{2}$ tsp) dried

1 bay leaf

1 garlic clove, skinned and crushed

15 ml (1 tbsp) tomato purée

1.7 litres (3 pints) stock

salt and freshly ground pepper

125 g (4 oz) macaroni, rigatoni or
   penne

4 slices of wholemeal bread

50 g (2 oz) Edam cheese, coarsely
   grated

basil sprigs, to garnish

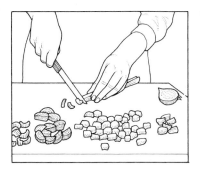

1 Cut the carrot, turnip, onion and celery into large dice.

2 Place the vegetables, thyme, basil, bay leaf and crushed garlic in a large saucepan. Stir over low heat for 2–3 minutes.

3 Stir in the tomato purée, stock and seasoning to taste. Bring to the boil, then lower the heat and simmer for 25–30 minutes.

4 Stir in the pasta. Cover and simmer for a further 12–15 minutes or until the pasta is tender. Taste and adjust the seasoning.

5 Toast the bread lightly on one side. Press a little cheese on to the untoasted side of the bread, dividing it equally between them. Grill until golden. Cut into small triangles.

6 Pour the soup into a warmed serving bowl. Serve immediately, garnished with the sprigs of basil and toasted cheese triangles.

——————— VARIATION ———————

Roughly chop 175 g (6 oz) smoked lean bacon and cook with the vegetables at the beginning of the recipe. Proceed as above.

SPINACH SOUP

0.30	50 cals

Serves 4

450 g (1 lb) fresh spinach

900 ml (1½ pints) vegetable or chicken stock

15 ml (1 tbsp) lemon juice

salt and freshly ground pepper

450 ml (¾ pint) buttermilk

a few drops of Tabasco sauce

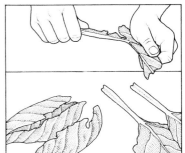

1 Strip the spinach leaves from their stems and wash in several changes of water. Place the spinach, stock, lemon juice and seasoning in a pan. Simmer for 10 minutes.

2 Work the spinach through a sieve, or strain off most of the liquid and reserve, then purée the spinach in a blender or processor.

3 Reheat the spinach purée gently with the cooking liquid, 300 ml (½ pint) of the buttermilk and Tabasco sauce. Swirl in the remaining buttermilk.

Menu Suggestion
Serve with warm wholemeal rolls.

CHILLED CUCUMBER SOUP

0.15* £ 92 cals

* plus 1 hour chilling

Serves 4

1 medium-sized cucumber, trimmed

300 ml (½ pint) natural yogurt

1 small garlic clove, skinned and crushed

30 ml (2 tbsp) wine vinegar

30 ml (2 tbsp) chopped fresh mint or snipped chives

salt and freshly ground pepper

300 ml (½ pint) milk

mint sprigs, to garnish

1 Grate the unpeeled cucumber into a bowl, using the finest side of a conical or box grater.

2 Stir in the yogurt, crushed garlic, vinegar and mint or chives. Add seasoning to taste and chill in the refrigerator for 1 hour.

3 Just before serving, stir in the milk, then taste and adjust seasoning. Spoon into individual soup bowls and garnish with sprigs of mint.

Menu Suggestion
This soup can be made in advance and served before the main course of a barbecue.

SMOKED MACKEREL WITH APPLE

| 0.20 | £ | 141 cals |

Serves 8

100 g (4 oz) celery, washed and trimmed

100 g (4 oz) cucumber, skinned

100 g (4 oz) red eating apple, cored

350 g (12 oz) smoked mackerel

150 ml (¼ pint) soured cream

30 ml (2 tbsp) lemon juice

paprika pepper

1 small crisp lettuce

lemon wedges, to serve (optional)

1 Finely chop the celery, cucumber and apple.

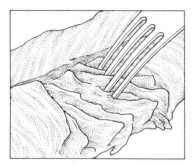

2 Skin the fish, then flake the flesh roughly with a fork. Discard the bones.

3 Combine the celery, cucumber, apple and mackerel in a bowl. Stir in the soured cream, lemon juice and paprika to taste.

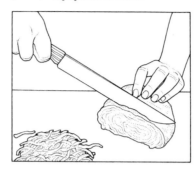

4 Shred the lettuce on a board with a sharp knife. Place a little lettuce in the bases of 8 stemmed glasses. Divide the mackerel equally between them.

5 Garnish each glass with a lemon wedge if liked, and sprinkle with paprika. Serve at room temperature.

Menu Suggestion

Serve with crusty bread as a starter or as part of a light salad lunch.

SMOKED MACKEREL WITH APPLE

There are two kinds of smoked mackerel available: hot-smoked and cold-smoked. Hot-smoked mackerel is the one most widely available, and it does not need cooking before eating, whereas cold-smoked mackerel does. When buying mackerel for this recipe, check with the fishmonger or packet instructions. Smoked fish of all kinds is first salted or soaked in a brine solution, and the length of time it is left at this stage will affect the flavour of the fish. Flavour is also affected by the actual smoking process itself; traditional methods use peat, oak chippings or other similar aromatic woods, but some modern smoking methods in factories use synthetic flavourings—and colourings too.

KIPPER MOUSSE

0.20* £ 192 cals

*plus 1 hour chilling

Serves 4

350 g (12 oz) kipper fillets
juice of 1 orange
15 ml (1 tbsp) lemon juice
5 ml (1 tsp) gelatine
100 g (4 oz) cottage or curd cheese
150 ml ($\frac{1}{4}$ pint) natural yogurt
1 small garlic clove, skinned and
   crushed
1.25 ml ($\frac{1}{4}$ tsp) ground mace
salt and freshly ground pepper
lemon or orange slices and herb
   sprigs, to garnish

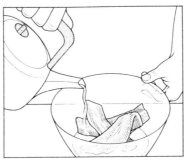

1 Pour boiling water over the kippers and leave to stand for 1 minute. Drain, pat dry and remove the skin. Flake the flesh, discarding any bones, and put into a blender or food processor.

2 In a small heatproof bowl, mix the orange and lemon juices together. Sprinkle on the gelatine and leave to stand for a few minutes until spongy.

3 Meanwhile, add the cottage cheese, yogurt, garlic and mace to the blender or food processor and blend until smooth.

4 Place the bowl of gelatine in a saucepan of hot water and heat gently until dissolved. Add to the kipper mixture and blend until evenly mixed. Season to taste.

5 Divide the kipper mousse equally between 6 oiled individual ramekin dishes. Chill in the refrigerator for at least 1 hour before serving.

6 Turn the mousses out on to individual plates and garnish.

Menu Suggestion
These tangy fish mousses can be served as part of a light lunch, or as a starter to any main meal. Serve with wholemeal toast.

KIPPER MOUSSE
Kippers are herrings which have been split and cold-smoked, that is they need to be cooked before eating—standing them in boiling water for a minute or so is the traditional, and best, method. When buying kippers, check for plump flesh and an oily skin— these are signs of quality. A dark-brown colour does not necessarily mean a good kipper, as this is probably an artificial dye. Some of the best kippers are the undyed Manx variety — available from good fishmongers.

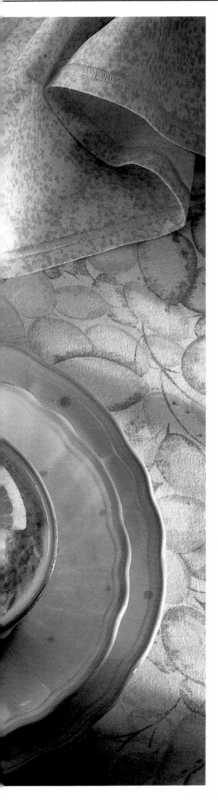

MARINATED MUSHROOMS

0.15*	76 cals

* plus 6–8 hours marinating

Serves 4

450 g (1 lb) small button
   mushrooms, wiped
30 ml (2 tbsp) wine vinegar
90 ml (6 tbsp) sunflower oil
pinch of mustard powder
pinch of Barbados sugar
salt and freshly ground pepper
chopped fresh parsley, to garnish

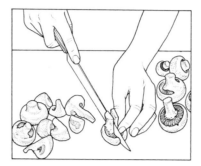

1 Trim the mushrooms. Leave small mushrooms whole and cut larger ones in quarters.

2 Put the vinegar, oil, mustard and sugar in a bowl with seasoning to taste. Whisk together with a fork until well blended.

3 Add the mushrooms and stir to coat in the marinade. Cover and leave to marinate in the refrigerator for 6–8 hours, stirring occasionally.

4 Taste and adjust the seasoning of the mushrooms, then divide equally between 4 individual shallow serving dishes. Sprinkle with chopped parsley and serve immediately.

Menu Suggestion
Marinated mushrooms make a refreshingly light start to a substantial main course. Serve with crusty brown bread to mop up the juices.

BUTTER BEAN PÂTÉ

2.30* £ ✳ 151–202 cals

* plus overnight soaking

Serves 6–8

225 g (8 oz) dried butter beans,
  soaked in cold water overnight

60 ml (4 tbsp) olive oil

juice of 2 lemons

2 garlic cloves, skinned and
  crushed

30 ml (2 tbsp) chopped fresh
  coriander

salt and freshly ground pepper

coriander sprigs and black olives,
  to garnish

1 Drain the butter beans into a
sieve and rinse thoroughly
under cold running water. Put in a
saucepan, cover with cold water
and bring to the boil.

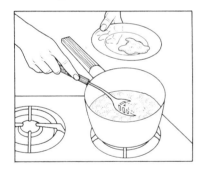

2 With a slotted spoon, skim off
any scum that rises to the
surface. Half cover the pan with a
lid and simmer for 1½–2 hours
until the beans are very tender.

3 Drain the beans and rinse
under cold running water. Put
half of the beans in a blender or
food processor with half of the oil,
lemon juice, garlic and coriander.
Blend to a smooth purée, then
transfer to a bowl. Repeat with the
remaining beans, oil, lemon juice,
garlic and coriander.

4 Beat the 2 batches of purée
together until well mixed, then
add seasoning to taste.

5 Turn the pâté into a serving
bowl and rough up the surface
with the prongs of a fork. Garnish
with the coriander and black
olives. Chill in the refrigerator
until serving time.

Menu Suggestion

Serve this creamy dip with fingers
of hot wholemeal pitta bread or
granary toast for an informal
supper party starter.

——— VARIATION ———

If you want to make this dip really
quickly, use two 396 g (14 oz) cans
butter beans and start the recipe
from the beginning of step 3.

AVOCADO AND GARLIC DIP WITH CRUDITÉS

| 0.30* | 208–312 cals |

* plus a maximum of 2 hours chilling

Serves 4–6

2 ripe avocados

juice of 1 lemon

225 g (8 oz) low-fat soft cheese

2 large garlic cloves, skinned and crushed

dash of Tabasco sauce, to taste

salt and freshly ground pepper

4 carrots

4 celery sticks

225 g (8 oz) cauliflower florets

100 g (4 oz) button mushrooms, wiped

8 cherry tomatoes or large radishes

1 Cut the avocados in half, then twist the halves in opposite directions to separate them. Remove the stones.

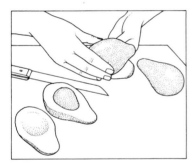

2 With a teaspoon, scoop the avocado flesh from the shells into a bowl.

3 Mash the avocado flesh with a fork, adding half of the lemon juice to prevent discoloration.

4 Whisk in the cheese and garlic until evenly mixed, then add Tabasco and seasoning to taste.

5 Transfer the dip to a serving bowl. Cover tightly with cling film, then chill in the refrigerator until serving time (but no longer than 2 hours).

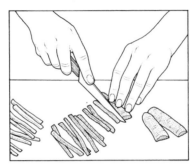

6 Before serving, prepare the vegetables. Scrape the carrots and cut them into thin sticks. Trim the celery and scrub clean under cold running water, then cut into thin sticks. Wash the cauliflower and separate into bite-sized florets. Toss the mushrooms in the remaining lemon juice.

7 To serve. Uncover the dip and place the bowl in the centre of a large serving platter and surround with the prepared vegetables. Serve immediately or the avocado in the dip may discolour.

Menu Suggestion

Serve for informal "nibbles" with drinks before you and your guests sit down to dinner.

MELON AND PRAWN SALAD

0.20* £ £ 133 cals

* plus 1 hour chilling

Serves 8

1 small honeydew melon

30 ml (2 tbsp) tomato juice

30 ml (2 tbsp) cider vinegar

30 ml (2 tbsp) clear honey

1 egg yolk

450 g (1 lb) peeled prawns

225 g (8 oz) cucumber, diced

15 ml (1 tbsp) chopped fresh
tarragon or 5 ml (1 tsp) dried

salt and freshly ground pepper

tarragon sprigs and 8 large whole
cooked prawns, to garnish

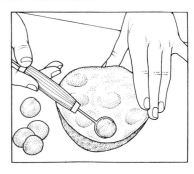

2 Scoop out the melon flesh with a melon baller. Divide the melon balls equally between 8 individual serving dishes.

3 Make the tomato dressing. Put the tomato juice, vinegar, honey and egg yolk in a blender or food processor and blend together until evenly mixed.

4 Toss the prawns, cucumber and tarragon in the tomato dressing. Add seasoning to taste. Spoon on top of the melon balls and chill in the refrigerator for at least 1 hour. Garnish with sprigs of tarragon and whole prawns before serving.

Menu Suggestion
The combination of shellfish and fruit in a piquant herb dressing makes an unusual start for a dinner party.

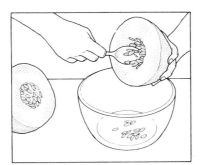

1 Cut the melon in half and scrape out the pips from the centre with a teaspoon.

MELON AND PRAWN SALAD

The honeydew melon used in this recipe is perhaps the best known of all the melons. The skin of the honeydew is bright yellow and the flesh pale green, with a sweet and juicy flesh. Honeydews are widely available—most of them come from Spain and Israel—but take care when buying as they can be watery and insipid at certain times of year. To test if a honeydew is at the correct degree of ripeness, first hold it in your hand: it should feel heavy. Secondly, press gently at both ends: the skin should give slightly under the pressure of your thumb, but not be too soft or squidgy, which is an indication that the melon is past its best.

Lunches, Snacks and Suppers

For quick meals and snacks, many of us rely on convenience foods: either frozen or canned — or even take-away 'junk' food. In this chapter you will find lots of ideas for nutritious quick meals which will make you think twice about opening a can. Burgers, pizza, stuffed baked potatoes, and pasta are all here, but these are the homemade kind. They taste fresher and have far more flavour — and you can be sure of knowing exactly what goes into them.

CHICKEN LIVER SKEWERS

| 0.30 | 🍴 | £ | 267 cals |

Serves 4

2 small oranges

200 ml (7 fl oz) unsweetened orange
   juice

5 ml (1 tsp) chopped fresh tarragon
   or 2.5 ml ($\frac{1}{2}$ tsp) dried

450 g (1 lb) whole chicken livers

2 slices of bread, crumbed

margarine or butter

1 green pepper, about 175 g (6 oz),
   seeded and roughly chopped

100 g (4 oz) onion, skinned and
   roughly chopped

275 g (10 oz) beansprouts

1 small bunch of chives, snipped

salt and freshly ground pepper

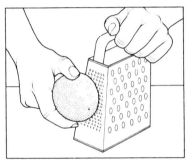

1 Finely grate the rind of 1 of
the oranges. Place in a saucepan with the orange juice and
tarragon and simmer for 2–3
minutes until reduced by half.

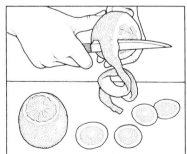

2 Cut the tops and bottoms off
both oranges, then remove the
skin by working around oranges
in a spiral, using a sharp
serrated knife and a sawing action.

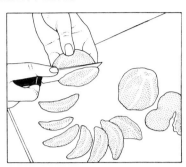

3 Divide the oranges into
segments by cutting through
the membranes on either side of
each segment with a sharp knife.

4 Cut the chicken livers in half;
toss lightly in the breadcrumbs. Place in a lightly greased
grill pan and grill for 2 minutes on
each side or until just firm.

5 Thread the pepper and onion
on to 4 oiled kebab skewers
alternately with the livers.

6 Place the skewers in the grill
pan and spoon over a little of
the reduced orange juice. Grill for
2–3 minutes on each side, turning
and basting occasionally.

7 Meanwhile, steam the beansprouts for 2–3 minutes (see
page 149). Warm the orange segments in a separate pan with the
remaining reduced orange juice.

8 Mix the beansprouts with the
chives and seasoning to taste,
and arrange on a warmed serving
dish. Top with the skewers and
spoon over the orange and juices.
Serve immediately.

Menu Suggestion
Chicken liver skewers are quick
and easy to make for a family meal
or impromptu entertaining. All
you need to accompany them is a
quickly cooked colourful vegetable
such as stir-fry mange-tout.

WHOLEWHEAT MACARONI BAKE

| 0.50 | £ ✳* | 273–410 cals |

* freeze at the end of step 7

Serves 4–6

175 g (6 oz) wholewheat macaroni

salt and freshly ground pepper

30 ml (2 tbsp) vegetable oil

1 onion, skinned and chopped

225 g (8 oz) button mushrooms, wiped

350 g (12 oz) tomatoes, skinned and roughly chopped

300 ml ($\frac{1}{2}$ pint) vegetable stock

15 ml (1 tbsp) tomato purée

5 ml (1 tsp) dried mixed herbs

5 ml (1 tsp) dried oregano

30 ml (2 tbsp) wholewheat flour

300 ml ($\frac{1}{2}$ pint) milk

100 g (4 oz) low-fat soft cheese

1 egg, beaten

5 ml (1 tsp) English mustard powder

30 ml (2 tbsp) wholewheat breadcrumbs

30 ml (2 tbsp) grated Parmesan cheese

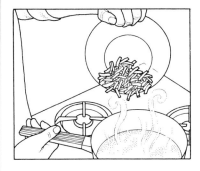

1 Plunge the macaroni into a large saucepan of boiling salted water. Simmer, uncovered, for 10 minutes.

2 Meanwhile, heat the oil in a separate pan, add the onion and fry gently for 5 minutes until soft but not coloured.

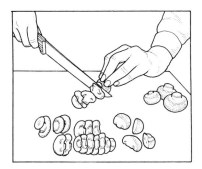

3 Cut the small mushrooms in half, slice the larger ones. Add to the pan, increase the heat and toss with the onion for 1–2 minutes until the juices run.

4 Add the tomatoes and stock and bring to the boil, stirring constantly to break up the tomatoes. Lower the heat, add the tomato purée, herbs and seasoning to taste, and simmer gently for 10 minutes.

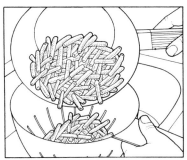

5 Drain the macaroni into a colander and leave to stand while making the cheese sauce.

6 Put the flour and milk in a blender or food processor and blend for 1 minute. Transfer to a heavy-based pan and simmer, stirring constantly, for 5 minutes until thickened. Remove from the heat and beat in the cheese, egg, mustard and seasoning to taste.

7 Mix the macaroni with the mushrooms in tomato sauce, then pour into a baking dish. Pour the cheese sauce over the top and sprinkle with the breadcrumbs and Parmesan.

8 Bake in the oven at 190°C (375°F) mark 5 for 20 minutes until golden brown and bubbling. Serve hot, straight from the dish.

Menu Suggestion

This supper dish is so substantial that it needs no accompaniment. Follow with a green salad to refresh the palate, then fresh fruit and cheese.

WHOLEWHEAT MACARONI BAKE

Wholewheat macaroni is now widely available from super-markets and health food shops. It is made from 100 per cent wholewheat flour and therefore has more fibre than ordinary white varieties. The flavour of wholewheat macaroni is pleasantly nutty and the texture quite firm—check with packet instructions for exact cooking times of each brand, because many of them tend to be longer than for white pasta. In Italy, wholewheat pasta is rarely seen and the short-cut or elbow macaroni that we are used to is not so common. Italian *maccheroni* tubes vary in length and thickness from one manu-facturer to another. Other types of Italian pasta similar to *maccheroni* which you may see in the shops are *penne* and *rigatoni*.

TAGLIATELLE WITH CHEESE AND NUT SAUCE

0.15	770 cals

Serves 4

400 g (14 oz) wholewheat or green (spinach) tagliatelle

salt and freshly ground pepper

100 g (4 oz) Gorgonzola cheese

100 g (4 oz) walnuts, chopped

5 ml (1 tsp) chopped fresh sage or 2.5 ml ($\frac{1}{2}$ tsp) dried sage

75 ml (5 tbsp) olive oil

15 ml (1 tbsp) chopped fresh parsley, to garnish

1 Plunge the tagliatelle into a large saucepan of boiling salted water. Simmer, uncovered, for 10 minutes or according to packet instructions, until *al dente* (tender but firm to the bite).

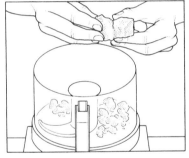

2 Meanwhile, crumble the cheese into a blender or food processor. Add two-thirds of the walnuts and the sage. Blend to combine the ingredients.

3 Add the oil gradually through the funnel (as when making mayonnaise) and blend until the sauce is evenly incorporated.

4 Drain the tagliatelle well and return to the pan. Add the nut sauce and fold in gently to mix. Add seasoning to taste.

5 Transfer the pasta and sauce to a warmed serving bowl and sprinkle with the remaining walnuts. Serve immediately garnished with chopped parsley.

Menu Suggestion
Quick to make at the last-minute, this nutritious dish makes an unusual lunch or supper. Serve with a crisp green salad tossed in a lemony vinaigrette dressing.

TAGLIATELLE WITH CHEESE AND NUT SAUCE

The Gorgonzola cheese used to make the sauce for this pasta dish must be one of the world's best-known blue cheeses. Real Gorgonzola cheese comes from the town of the same name in Lombardy, northern Italy. Originally it was made in the damp caves there, but nowadays it is mostly made in factories. The unique piquant flavour and creamy paste of Gorgonzola were produced naturally by the damp atmosphere in the caves, but in factories a similar result is achieved by using a bacteria known as *penicillium gorgonzola*. The process of making the cheese can now take as little as three months—as opposed to the twelve months taken by the traditional method.

SPAGHETTI WITH RATATOUILLE SAUCE

| 1.10 | £ ✳* | 458 cals |

* freeze the ratatouille sauce separately at the end of step 6

Serves 4

1 aubergine
salt and freshly ground pepper
1 onion, skinned
1 garlic clove, skinned
1 green pepper
1 red pepper
3 medium courgettes
350 g (12 oz) tomatoes
10 ml (2 tsp) chopped fresh basil
400 g (14 oz) wholewheat spaghetti
freshly grated Parmesan cheese, to serve

1 Dice the aubergine, then spread out on a plate and sprinkle with salt. Dégorge for 30 minutes until the juices flow.

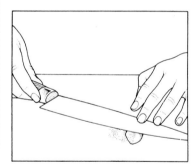

2 Meanwhile, prepare the remaining vegetables for the ratatouille sauce. Chop the onion finely. Crush the garlic on a board with a little salt and the flat of the blade of a large cook's knife.

3 Cut the peppers in half, remove the cores and seeds and wash well. Slice the flesh into thin strips.

4 Top and tail the courgettes, then slice them into very thin strips, leaving the skin on.

5 Skin the tomatoes. Put them in a heatproof bowl and pour in boiling water to cover. Leave to stand for 2 minutes, then drain and plunge into a bowl of cold water. Remove from the water one at a time, then peel off the skin with your fingers. Chop the flesh of the tomatoes finely.

6 Tip the diced aubergine into a sieve and rinse under cold running water. Put into a large, heavy-based pan with the prepared vegetables, basil and seasoning to taste. Cover and cook over moderate heat for 30 minutes. Shake the pan and stir the vegetables frequently during this time, to encourage the juices to flow.

7 Meanwhile, plunge the spaghetti into a separate large saucepan of boiling salted water. Simmer, uncovered, for 12 minutes or according to packet instructions, until *al dente* (tender but firm to the bite).

8 Drain the spaghetti thoroughly and turn into a warmed serving dish. Taste and adjust the seasoning of the ratatouille sauce, then pour over the spaghetti. Serve immediately, with the Parmesan cheese handed separately.

Menu Suggestion
The wholewheat spaghetti and rich, vegetable sauce together make this dish a complete meal.

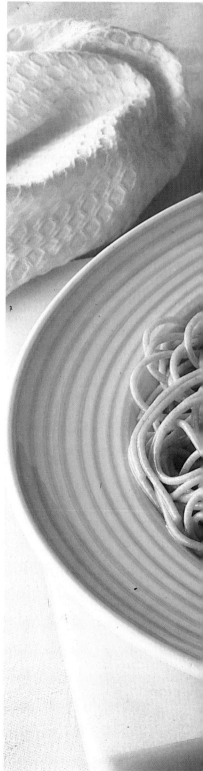

PRAWN RISOTTO

| 0.45 | £ £ | 293 cals |

Serves 4

75 g (3 oz) onion, skinned and thinly sliced

1 garlic clove, skinned and crushed

1 litre (1¾ pints) chicken stock

225 g (8 oz) long grain brown rice

50 g (2 oz) small button mushrooms

½ sachet saffron threads

salt and freshly ground pepper

225 g (8 oz) peeled prawns

50 g (2 oz) frozen petits pois

12 whole prawns, to garnish

1 Place the onion, garlic, stock, rice, mushrooms and saffron in a large saucepan or flameproof casserole. Add seasoning to taste. Bring to the boil and simmer, uncovered, for 35 minutes, stirring occasionally.

2 Stir in the prawns and petits pois. Cook over high heat for about 5 minutes, stirring occasionally until most of the liquid has been absorbed.

3 Taste and adjust the seasoning, then turn into a warmed serving dish. Garnish with the whole prawns and serve immediately.

Menu Suggestion
This succulent risotto made with brown rice and prawns would be perfectly offset by a tomato, onion and basil salad.

BAKED POTATOES WITH CHICK PEAS

| 1.50 | f | 492 cals |

Serves 4

4 baking potatoes, each weighing about 275 g (10 oz)

45 ml (3 tbsp) vegetable oil

salt and freshly ground pepper

1 medium onion, skinned and roughly chopped

2.5 ml ($\frac{1}{2}$ tsp) ground coriander

2.5 ml ($\frac{1}{2}$ tsp) ground cumin

400 g (14 oz) can chick peas, drained

60 ml (4 tbsp) chopped fresh parsley

150 ml ($\frac{1}{4}$ pint) natural yogurt

chopped fresh parsley, to garnish

1 Scrub the potatoes and pat dry. Brush them with 15 ml (1 tbsp) of the vegetable oil and sprinkle lightly with salt.

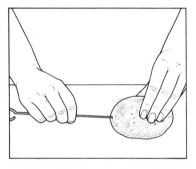

2 Run thin skewers through the potatoes to help conduct the heat through them. Place them directly on the oven shelves and bake in the oven at 200°C (400°F) mark 6 for 1$\frac{1}{4}$ hours until tender.

3 Meanwhile, heat remaining oil in a large saucepan, add the onion, coriander and cumin and fry for 4 minutes, stirring occasionally. Add the chick peas and cook for a further 1–2 minutes, stirring all the time.

4 Halve the potatoes and scoop out the flesh, keeping the shells intact. Add the potato flesh to the chick pea mixture with the parsley and yogurt. Mash until smooth; add seasoning to taste.

5 Place the potato shells on a baking sheet and fill with the potato and chick pea mixture. Return to the oven and bake for a further 10–15 minutes. Serve hot sprinkled with chopped parsley.

Menu Suggestion
Serve with a salad of shredded cabbage, celery, apple and walnuts.

CRUNCHY BAKED POTATO SKINS

| 1.40 | £ | 198 cals |

Serves 4

4 medium baking potatoes
60 ml (4 tbsp) vegetable oil
salt and freshly ground pepper
300 ml ($\frac{1}{2}$ pint) natural yogurt
30 ml (2 tbsp) snipped chives

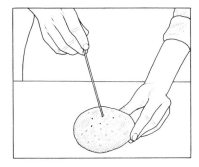

1 Pierce the potatoes all over with a skewer, then place directly on the oven shelf. Bake in the oven at 200°C (400°F) mark 6 for 1$\frac{1}{4}$ hours until tender.

2 Cut each potato in half length-ways and scoop out most of the flesh with a sharp-edged teaspoon, taking care not to split the skins.

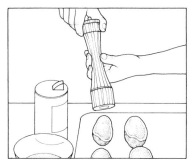

3 Stand the potato skins on a lightly oiled baking sheet. Brush them inside and out with the oil and sprinkle with plenty of salt and freshly ground pepper.

4 Increase the oven temperature to 220°C (425°F) mark 7 and bake for 10 minutes until crisp.

5 Meanwhile, whisk the yogurt and chives together with seasoning to taste. Spoon into a serving bowl or sauceboat.

6 Serve the potato skins piping hot, with the yogurt dressing handed separately.

Menu Suggestion
Crunchy baked potato skins are an American idea. Put a spoonful or two of dressing in each potato skin and either eat with the fingers as the Americans do, or with a knife and fork if you prefer. Apart from making a quick and easy snack, they are also good served as a starter before spareribs or burgers.

WHOLEWHEAT SPINACH PANCAKES

| 0.40 | ✳* | 313 cals |

* freeze pancakes only at the end of step 7

Serves 4

175 g (6 oz) fresh spinach, washed
100 g (4 oz) wholewheat flour
salt and freshly ground pepper
150 ml (¼ pint) milk
150 ml (¼ pint) water
1 egg, beaten
about 45 ml (3 tbsp) vegetable oil, for frying
225 g (8 oz) cottage cheese with prawns
2.5 ml (½ tsp) paprika
whole prawns and sprigs of herbs, to garnish

1 Cut away the thick midribs and stalks from the spinach and put the leaves in a saucepan with only the water that clings to them. Cover and cook gently for 5 minutes until tender.

2 Drain the spinach in a colander, pressing down with a spoon to extract as much water as possible from the leaves.

3 Turn the spinach on to a board and chop very finely with a sharp knife.

4 Put the flour in a bowl with a pinch of salt. Make a well in the centre, add half of the milk and water and the egg.

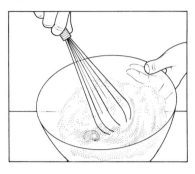

5 Beat vigorously with a whisk, gradually incorporating the flour into the centre. Whisk in the remaining liquid and the spinach.

6 Heat a little oil in a pancake pan or heavy-based 18 cm (7 inch) frying pan. Pour the batter into a jug and whisk.

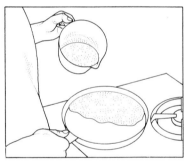

7 Pour one-eighth of the batter into the pan and tip and tilt the pan so that the batter runs all over the base. Cook over moderate heat for about 30 seconds until the underside is golden, then turn the pancake over and repeat cooking on the other side.

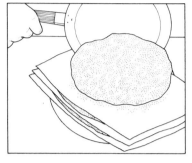

8 Slide the pancake out on to a sheet of greaseproof paper placed over a plate and keep warm while cooking the remaining 7 pancakes. (As each pancake is made, stack it on top of the last one, with greaseproof in between.)

9 Season the cottage cheese with the paprika and salt and pepper to taste. Spread a little over each pancake, then roll up or fold into parcels. Serve immediately garnished with the prawns and herbs.

Menu Suggestion
Serve for lunch with a tomato and onion salad.

CURRIED NUT BURGERS

0.50* ✳* 744 cals

* plus 30 minutes chilling; freeze after coating in step 5

Makes 6

90 ml (6 tbsp) vegetable oil

1 onion, skinned and finely chopped

15 ml (1 tbsp) Madras curry paste or powder

175 g (6 oz) Edam cheese, diced

175 g (6 oz) chopped mixed nuts

175 g (6 oz) granary breadcrumbs

2 carrots, peeled and grated

salt and freshly ground pepper

2 eggs

30 ml (2 tbsp) wholewheat flour, to coat

watercress sprigs, radicchio and cucumber, to garnish

1 Heat 30 ml (2 tbsp) of the oil in a small saucepan, add the onion and curry paste or powder and fry gently for 5 minutes until the onion is soft but not coloured.

2 Put the onion in a bowl with the cheese, 150 g (5 oz) of the nuts and 125 g (4 oz) of the bread-crumbs. Add the carrots and seasoning to taste, and stir well to mix. Bind with one of the eggs.

3 With floured hands, form the mixture into 6 burger shapes, coating them lightly with flour.

4 Beat the remaining egg in a shallow dish and dip the burgers in it to coat them lightly.

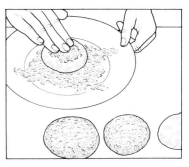

5 Mix the remaining nuts and breadcrumbs together on a flat plate. Coat the burgers in this mixture, pressing on firmly with your hands. Chill the burgers in the refrigerator for 30 minutes to firm the coating.

6 Heat the remaining oil in a large frying pan, add the burgers and fry over moderate to high heat for 10 minutes on each side until golden brown and cooked through. Drain on absorbent kitchen paper before serving with the watercress, radicchio and cucumber.

Menu Suggestion

Serve these burgers hot or cold, with wedges of lemon or lime. A natural yogurt, cucumber and mint salad would make a refreshing accompaniment, contrasting well with the spicy richness of the curried nut mixture.

CHILLI PIZZA FINGERS

1.00 ☐ £ ✳ 461 cals

Serves 6

225 g (8 oz) minced beef

2.5 ml (½ tsp) chilli powder

1 garlic clove, skinned and crushed

1 medium onion, skinned and chopped

1 small green pepper, cored, seeded and chopped

100 g (4 oz) mushrooms, wiped and sliced

225 g (8 oz) tomatoes, skinned and chopped

213 g (7.51 oz) can red kidney beans, drained

150 ml (¼ pint) beef stock

225 g (8 oz) plain wholewheat flour

50 g (2 oz) medium oatmeal

15 ml (1 tbsp) baking powder

salt and freshly ground pepper

50 g (2 oz) margarine or butter

1 egg, beaten

60 ml (4 tbsp) milk

15 ml (1 tbsp) tomato purée

175 g (6 oz) Mozzarella cheese, thinly sliced

basil sprigs, to garnish

1 First prepare the topping. Place the minced beef, chilli powder and garlic in a saucepan and fry for 3–4 minutes, stirring occasionally. Add the onion, green pepper and mushrooms and fry for a further 1–2 minutes. Stir in the tomatoes, red kidney beans and beef stock. Bring to the boil and simmer for about 15 minutes, stirring occasionally until most of the liquid has evaporated.

2 Meanwhile, combine the flour, oatmeal, baking powder and a pinch of salt in a bowl.

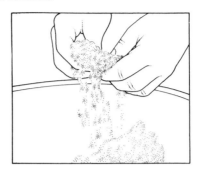

3 Rub in the margarine until the mixture resembles fine breadcrumbs. Bind to a soft dough with the egg and milk, then turn out on to a floured surface and knead lightly until smooth.

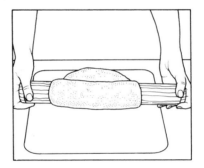

4 Roll out the dough to a 25 × 18 cm (10 × 7 inch) rectangle. Lift on to a baking sheet, then spread carefully with tomato purée. Pile the chilli mixture on top and cover with Mozzarella cheese.

5 Bake in the oven at 200°C (400°F) mark 6 for about 30 minutes until golden and bubbling. Cut into fingers for serving, garnished with basil sprigs.

Menu Suggestion
Serve as a substantial snack, or an easy supper dish accompanied by a salad of thinly sliced or grated courgettes dressed with a vinaigrette and snipped fresh chives.

MUSHROOM FLAN

| 0.45 | £ | 303 cals |

Serves 4

100 g (4 oz) wholewheat breadcrumbs

300 ml ($\frac{1}{2}$ pint) natural yogurt

salt and freshly ground pepper

4 eggs

150 ml ($\frac{1}{4}$ pint) milk

175 g (6 oz) mushrooms, wiped and sliced

4 spring onions, trimmed and chopped

75 g (3 oz) Cheddar cheese, grated

1 Mix the breadcrumbs and 150 ml ($\frac{1}{4}$ pint) of the yogurt to a paste. Add seasoning to taste.

2 Use the mixture to line a 23 cm (9 inch) flan dish or tin, pressing the paste into shape with the fingers. Set aside.

3 Whisk the eggs and milk together with the remaining yogurt and seasoning to taste.

4 Arrange the mushrooms, spring onions and half the cheese on the base of the flan. Pour the egg mixture over the top and then sprinkle with the remaining cheese.

5 Bake the flan in the oven at 180°C (350°F) mark 4 for about 30 minutes or until brown and set. Serve warm.

Menu Suggestion

This cheesy mushroom flan is best served with a colourful salad such as a mixture of sweetcorn, green pepper and onion.

MUSHROOM FLAN

The unusual base for this flan is made simply from wholewheat breadcrumbs and yogurt—less fattening than a conventional shortcrust pastry base—and with healthier ingredients. If you prefer to use a pastry base, however, then use your own favourite recipe, or try the following recipe for wholewheat pastry, which is sufficient to line a 23 cm (9 inch) flan dish. Mix 175 g (6 oz) wholewheat flour and a pinch of salt in a bowl, add 40 g (1$\frac{1}{2}$ oz) each butter or margarine and lard in small pieces and rub in with the fingertips until the mixture resembles fine crumbs. Sprinkle about 40 ml (8 tsp) ice-cold water into the bowl and mix it in with a knife. Draw the mixture together with the fingers of one hand, then chill or leave to rest for 30 minutes.

PERSIAN OMELETTE

| 0.40 | 308 cals |

Serves 4

450 g (1 lb) fresh spinach or
   226 g (8 oz) packet frozen spinach

225 g (8 oz) potatoes, peeled

45 ml (3 tbsp) vegetable oil

1 medium onion, skinned and
   chopped

4 eggs, beaten

salt and freshly ground pepper

grated rind of $\frac{1}{2}$ lemon

juice of 1 lemon

1 If using fresh spinach, wash, and while still wet, place in a saucepan. Cover and cook gently for 5 minutes until tender.

2 Drain well and chop finely. If using frozen spinach, place in a saucepan and cook for 7–10 minutes to drive off as much liquid as possible.

3 Cut the potato into small dice. Heat the 30 ml (2 tbsp) of the oil in a 20.5 cm (8 inch) non-stick frying pan, add the potato and fry gently for 5 minutes until just turning brown. Add the onion and cook for about 10 minutes until golden. The potato should be almost tender. Remove from the heat and set aside.

4 In a large bowl, mix the spinach with the eggs, seasoning, lemon rind and juice. Add the potato and onion and mix well.

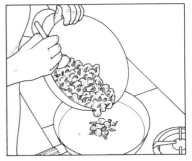

5 Heat the remaining oil in the same frying pan, pour in the egg mixture, spreading it evenly over the bottom of the pan. Cover with a lid or foil and cook gently for 15 minutes until just set.

6 Remove the lid or foil and brown under a hot grill before serving. Serve warm.

Menu Suggestion
All this substantial omelette needs as an accompaniment is crusty bread and a green salad.

LENTIL CROQUETTES

1.10* £ ✳* 183 cals

* plus 1 hour chilling; freeze after
shaping in step 5

Makes 8

225 g (8 oz) split red lentils

2 celery sticks, trimmed and
finely chopped

1 onion, skinned and chopped

1–2 garlic cloves, skinned and
crushed

600 ml (1 pint) water

10 ml (2 tsp) garam masala

1 egg, beaten

salt and freshly ground pepper

30 ml (2 tbsp) wholewheat flour,
to coat

5 ml (1 tsp) paprika

5 ml (1 tsp) ground turmeric

60 ml (4 tbsp) vegetable oil

fresh coriander or parsley and
lime wedges, to garnish

1 Place the lentils in a large
saucepan with the celery,
onion, garlic, water and garam
masala. Bring to the boil, stirring
with a wooden spoon to mix.

2 Lower the heat and simmer
gently for 30 minutes or until
the lentils are tender and have
absorbed all the liquid. Stir
frequently to prevent the lentils
sticking to the bottom of the pan.

3 Remove from the heat. Leave
to cool for a few minutes, then
beat in the egg and seasoning to
taste.

4 Turn the mixture on to a board
or flat plate and spread out
evenly. Leave until cold, then chill
in the refrigerator for 30 minutes
to firm the mixture.

5 With floured hands, form the
mixture into 8 triangular
croquette shapes. Coat in the flour
mixed with the paprika and
turmeric. Chill again 30 minutes.

6 Heat the oil in a large frying
pan, add the croquettes and
fry over moderate to high heat for
10 minutes, turning once until
crisp and golden on both sides.

7 Drain on absorbent kitchen
paper and serve hot, with a
sprinkling of chopped coriander or
parsley on top of each and lime
wedges.

Menu Suggestion
Serve these spicy croquettes for a
tasty lunch dish with a side salad
of tomato, onion and fennel, or a
crisp and crunchy coleslaw made
with grated raw white cabbage,
carrot, onion, apple and a yogurt
dressing (page 153).

CHILLED SMOKED TROUT WITH YOGURT AND ORANGE DRESSING

| 0.15* | £ £ | 199 cals |

* plus 30 minutes chilling

Serve 4

4 small smoked trout

**finely grated rind and juice of
1 orange**

150 ml ($\frac{1}{4}$ pint) natural yogurt

**5 ml (1 tsp) creamed horseradish
sauce**

salt and freshly ground pepper

**finely shredded lettuce or chicory
leaves, to serve**

orange segments, to garnish

1 Carefully remove the skin
from the trout, then divide
each fish into 2 fillets without
breaking them. Discard the bones.
Cover the fillets and chill in the
refrigerator for 30 minutes.

2 Meanwhile, mix the orange
rind, juice, yogurt and horseradish together. Season to taste.
Chill in the refrigerator for at least
30 minutes, with the smoked trout.

3 Cover 4 small serving plates
with the shredded lettuce or
chicory leaves. Carefully lay 2
fillets on each plate and spoon
over the dressing. Garnish with
the orange segments and serve
immediately.

Menu Suggestion
Serve with thin slices of lightly
buttered brown bread for a
summer lunch.

CHEESE, BEANSPROUT AND PINEAPPLE SALAD

0.15	£	211 cals

Serves 4

275 g (10 oz) beansprouts

225 g (8 oz) carrots, peeled

225 g (8 oz) Edam cheese

227 g (8 oz) can pineapple slices in natural juice

10 ml (2 tsp) wine vinegar

salt and freshly ground pepper

1 Wash the beansprouts. Drain well. Cut the carrots into 2.5 cm (1 inch) matchstick thin strips. Coarsely grate the cheese.

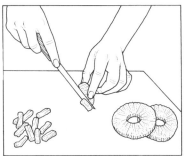

2 Drain the pineapple, reserving the juice. Cut the pineapple into thin strips.

3 In a large bowl, mix together the beansprouts, carrot, cheese and pineapple. Cover and chill in the refrigerator until required.

4 Make the dressing. Whisk the pineapple juice and vinegar together with seasoning to taste.

5 Just before serving, pour the dressing over the salad and toss well to mix. Serve at room temperature.

Menu Suggestion

This crisp and colourful salad can be served on its own or with warm cheese scones.

CHEESE, BEANSPROUT AND PINEAPPLE SALAD

Instead of the Edam cheese used here, use the same amount of tofu, available from the chilling cabinets in health food shops and some large supermarkets. Tofu is a curd made from soya beans—the beans are ground into an emulsion, then curdled with powdered gypsum (rather like rennet curdling milk). The Chinese have used tofu in their cooking for over 2000 years, and it is still eaten today all over China, Japan and East Asia for its health-giving properties. Weight for weight, tofu provides more first-class protein than steak, and for this reason it is extremely popular with vegetarians.

Main Courses

A good main course dish
should be satisfying
without being too filling.
If you use too many rich,
fatty ingredients or make
portions too generous,
this results in an
'overindulged' feeling.
Lean meat, fish, poultry
and fresh vegetables
form the basis for the
healthy and slim main
courses in this chapter,
giving you a wide
selection of low-fat
dishes, in which flavour
and freshness are brought
out to the full.

SLIMMERS' MOUSSAKA

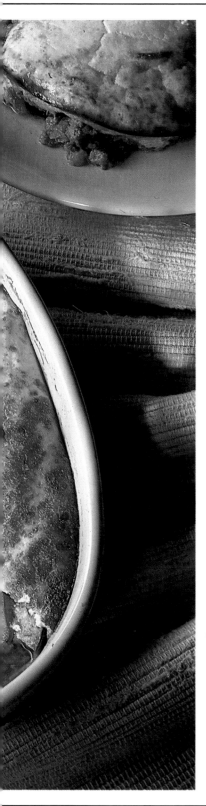

| 1.50* ⊟ £ ✳* | 362 cals |

* plus 30 minutes standing time; freeze at step 7, before baking

Serves 4

2 medium aubergines

salt and freshly ground pepper

450 g (1 lb) lean minced beef

2 medium onions, skinned and sliced

1 garlic clove, skinned and finely chopped

397 g (14 oz) can tomatoes

30 ml (2 tbsp) tomato purée

15 ml (1 tbsp) chopped fresh parsley

300 ml ($\frac{1}{2}$ pint) natural yogurt

2 eggs, beaten

pinch of grated nutmeg

15 ml (1 tbsp) grated Parmesan cheese

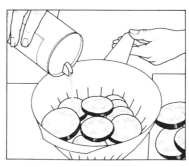

1 Thinly slice the aubergines, discarding the tops. Place in a colander, sprinkling each layer with salt. Cover with a plate, weight down and leave to stand for about 30 minutes.

2 Drain the aubergine slices, then rinse and dry well by patting with absorbent kitchen paper or a clean teatowel.

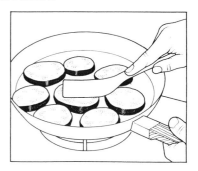

3 Cook the aubergine slices on both sides in a non-stick frying pan over high heat until brown, pressing the slices with the back of a spatula to release the moisture. Remove from the pan; set aside.

4 In the same pan, cook the meat for 5 minutes until browned, stirring and pressing with a wooden spoon to break up any lumps. Stir in the onions and cook for a further 5 minutes until lightly browned.

5 Add the garlic, tomatoes with their juice, the tomato purée, parsley and seasoning to taste. Bring to the boil, stirring, then lower the heat and simmer for 20 minutes until the meat is cooked.

6 Arrange a layer of aubergines in the bottom of an ovenproof dish. Spoon over the meat mixture, then finish with a layer of the remaining aubergines.

7 Beat the yogurt and eggs together with nutmeg and seasoning to taste. Pour over the dish and sprinkle with the grated Parmesan cheese.

8 Bake in the oven at 180°C (350°F) mark 4 for about 45 minutes until golden. Serve hot, straight from the dish.

Menu Suggestion
Serve with crusty granary bread and a green salad.

JAPANESE SKEWERED BEEF

0.25* £ £ ✳* 305 cals

* plus at least 8 hours marinating;
freeze in the marinade

Serves 4

700 g (1½ lb) fillet steak, trimmed
   of fat

5 cm (2 inch) piece fresh root
   ginger

2 garlic cloves

100 ml (4 fl oz) sake or dry sherry
   (see box)

60 ml (4 tbsp) soy sauce

30 ml (2 tbsp) sesame or vegetable
   oil

5 ml (1 tsp) soft brown sugar

carrot and cucumber slices,
   to garnish

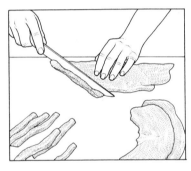

1 Cut the steak across the grain
into slices about 1 cm (½ inch)
thick, using a very sharp knife.

2 Skin the ginger and garlic.
Crush the flesh finely in a
mortar and pestle, or on a board
with the side of the blade of a
large cook's knife.

3 Put the crushed ginger and
garlic in a bowl with the sake,
soy sauce, oil and sugar. Whisk
with a fork until well combined,
then add the sliced steak and turn
to coat in the marinade. Cover and
leave to marinate for at least 8
hours, turning occasionally.

4 When ready to cook, thread
the slices of steak on to oiled
metal kebab skewers, or wooden
skewers that have been soaked for
30 minutes in water. Grill under
moderate heat for 5 minutes only,
turning frequently to ensure even
cooking and basting with the
marinade. Serve immediately
garnished with carrot slices and
cucumber.

Menu Suggestion
Eat these beef kebabs in Japanese
style on their own, followed by a
stir-fried dish of egg noodles,
beansprouts, mushrooms and
grated carrot.

JAPANESE SKEWERED BEEF

Sake is a wine made from rice.
Available in Japanese and other
oriental stores, it is used
extensively in the cooking of the
East—as well as being a
favourite potent drink. Although
described as 'rice wine', strictly
speaking it is not a wine because
it is not made from grapes.
Neither is it a spirit because it is
not distilled! Sake is made by
fermenting rice, and is usually
14–18% proof, so it tastes rather
strong. The Japanese drink it
warm in small porcelain bowls
called *sakazuki*, and if you eat
out in a Japanese restaurant you
are sure to be asked to try some.
For home cooking, a dry sherry
can be used as a substitute in
Japanese recipes, although its
flavour and bouquet will not be
so strong.

PAPRIKA BEEF

2.15 £ ✳ 213 cals

Serves 4

450 g (1 lb) lean shin of beef

15 ml (1 tbsp) plain wholewheat flour

7.5 ml (1½ tsp) mild paprika

1.25 ml (¼ tsp) caraway seeds

1.25 ml (¼ tsp) dried marjoram

salt and freshly ground pepper

175 g (6 oz) onion, skinned and sliced

225 g (8 oz) carrots, peeled and sliced

200 ml (7 fl oz) beef stock

15 ml (1 tbsp) tomato purée

1 garlic clove, skinned and crushed

1 whole clove

100 g (4 oz) button mushrooms, wiped and sliced

chopped fresh parsley, to garnish

1 Trim the fat from the beef. Cut the meat into chunky cubes. Mix together the flour, paprika, caraway seeds, marjoram and seasoning to taste. Toss the beef in the seasoned flour.

2 Layer the meat, onion and carrots in a 2 litre (3½ pint) flameproof casserole.

3 Whisk together the stock, tomato purée, crushed garlic and clove. Pour into the casserole. Bring to the boil and simmer, uncovered, for 3–4 minutes.

4 Cover the casserole tightly and cook in the oven at 180°C (350°F) mark 4 for about 1½ hours, stirring occasionally.

5 Remove the casserole from the oven and stir in the mushrooms. Cover again and return to the oven for a further 15 minutes or until the meat is tender. Taste and adjust seasoning. Garnish.

Menu Suggestion
Serve with layered sliced potatoes and onions, moistened with stock and baked in the oven.

MINTED LAMB MEATBALLS

| 1.20 | f | 201 cals |

Serves 4

225 g (8 oz) crisp cabbage, trimmed and finely chopped

450 g (1 lb) lean minced lamb

100 g (4 oz) onion, skinned and finely chopped

2.5 ml ($\frac{1}{2}$ tsp) ground allspice

salt and freshly ground pepper

397 g (14 oz) can tomato juice

1 bay leaf

10 ml (2 tsp) chopped fresh mint or 5 ml (1 tsp) dried

15 ml (1 tbsp) chopped fresh parsley

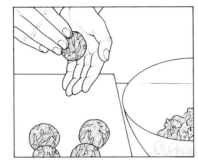

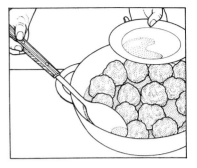

1 Steam the cabbage for 2–3 minutes or until softened (see page 149).

2 Place the lamb and cabbage in a bowl with the onion, allspice and seasoning to taste. Beat well to combine all the ingredients.

3 With your hands, shape the mixture into 16–20 small balls. Place the meatballs in a shallow large ovenproof dish.

4 Mix the tomato juice with the bay leaf, mint and parsley. Pour over the meatballs. Cover the dish tightly and bake in the oven at 180°C (350°F) mark 4 for about 1 hour until the meatballs are cooked.

5 Skim any fat off the tomato sauce before serving, and taste and adjust seasoning. Serve hot.

Menu Suggestion
Minted lamb meatballs are delicious served on a bed of steamed brown rice and followed by a crisp salad.

MARINATED LAMB KEBABS

0.30*	412 cals

* plus 1–2 days marinating

Serves 4

150 ml ($\frac{1}{4}$ pint) natural yogurt

2.5 cm (1 inch) piece fresh root ginger, peeled and grated

2 garlic cloves, skinned and crushed

30 ml (2 tbsp) chopped fresh mint

10 ml (2 tsp) crushed cumin seeds

5 ml (1 tsp) ground turmeric

5 ml (1 tsp) salt

2.5 ml ($\frac{1}{2}$ tsp) chilli powder

700 g (1$\frac{1}{2}$ lb) lean lamb shoulder, trimmed of excess fat and cut into cubes

2 medium onions

fresh mint sprigs and lemon wedges, to garnish

1 Put the yogurt in a large bowl and add the ginger, garlic, mint, cumin, turmeric, salt and chilli powder. Stir well to mix.

2 Add the cubes of lamb to the bowl and stir to coat in the marinade. Cover and refrigerate for 1–2 days, turning occasionally.

3 When ready to cook, skin the onions and cut into quarters with a sharp knife.

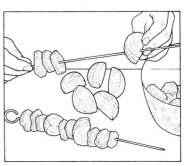

4 Thread the lamb and onion quarters alternately on to 4 oiled kebab skewers, pressing the pieces as close together as possible. Reserve any leftover marinade.

5 Grill the kebabs under moderate heat for 10 minutes until the lamb is browned on the outside and pink in the centre. Turn frequently during grilling and brush with the reserved marinade. Serve hot, garnished with mint and lemon wedges.

Menu Suggestion

Serve on a bed of brown rice with a Middle Eastern style salad of tomatoes, cucumber, chopped fresh mint and black olives.

MARINATED LAMB KEBABS

The marinating of the lamb in yogurt is an important stage, in this kebab recipe, so don't be tempted to skimp on the length of marinating time recommended. Natural yogurt contains a special bacteria which has the effect of tenderising meat and making it more succulent when cooked. The longer the meat is left in a yogurt marinade the more tender it will be—in the cookery of the Middle East, yogurt is frequently used for this purpose, especially with tough, sinewy cuts of meat.

LAMB CUTLETS WITH LEMON AND GARLIC

| 0.35 | £ £ | 502 cals |

Serves 4

2 lemons

3 small garlic cloves, skinned and crushed

salt and freshly ground pepper

8 lamb cutlets

30 ml (2 tbsp) vegetable oil

25 g (1 oz) margarine or butter

1 medium onion, skinned and finely chopped

175 ml (6 fl oz) natural yogurt

150 ml ($\frac{1}{4}$ pint) chicken stock

5 ml (1 tsp) chopped fresh basil or 2.5 ml ($\frac{1}{2}$ tsp) dried

parsley or basil sprigs, to garnish

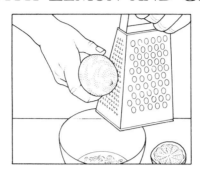

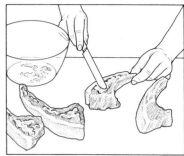

1 On the finest side of a conical or box grater, grate the rind of $1\frac{1}{2}$ lemons into a bowl. Add the garlic and freshly ground pepper to taste and blend together.

2 Place the cutlets on a board and spread the lemon rind and garlic evenly over the meat. Leave for 15 minutes.

3 Heat the oil and margarine in a pan, add the cutlets and fry for about 3 minutes each side or until tender. Drain and keep warm on a serving dish.

4 Pour off all but 30 ml (2 tbsp) fat from the pan, add the onion and fry gently for 5 minutes until soft but not coloured. Stir in the yogurt and stock with the squeezed juice of the $1\frac{1}{2}$ lemons and the basil. Bring to the boil and simmer for 2–3 minutes. Add salt and freshly ground pepper to taste.

5 Spoon the juices over the meat and garnish with the parsley or basil sprigs and the remaining $\frac{1}{2}$ lemon, cut into wedges, if liked. Serve immediately.

Menu Suggestion
Serve with French beans topped with grilled almonds and new potatoes in their skins.

APPLE BAKED CHOPS

1.30	✳	299 cals

Serves 4

225 g (8 oz) dessert apples

75 g (3 oz) onion, skinned

50 g (2 oz) raisins

200 ml (7 fl oz) unsweetened apple juice

45 ml (3 tbsp) chopped parsley

salt and freshly ground pepper

4 pork loin chops, about 175 g (6 oz) each, trimmed of fat

3 or 4 green cardamoms, lightly crushed

30 ml (2 tbsp) dry white wine or cider

parsley sprigs, to garnish

1 Core and finely chop the apple. Finely chop the onion. Place in a saucepan with the raisins and apple juice. Simmer gently, uncovered, for 3–4 minutes until the apple begins to soften slightly.

2 Remove from the heat, drain off the juices and reserve. Stir the parsley into the apple mixture with seasoning to taste, then cool.

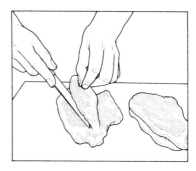

3 Meanwhile, make a horizontal cut through the flesh of the chops, almost to the bone. Open out to form a pocket for the apple.

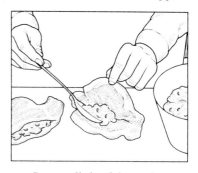

4 Spoon a little of the apple mixture into the pocket of each chop. Place in a shallow flame-proof dish. Sprinkle any remaining stuffing around the chops, with the crushed cardamoms. Mix the reserved juices with the wine or cider and pour over the chops.

5 Cover with foil and bake in the oven at 190°C (375°F) mark 5 for about 1 hour until tender.

6 Remove the chops from the dish and place in a grill pan. Grill until browned.

7 Meanwhile, pour the cooking juices from the chops into a pan and boil rapidly until reduced by half. Arrange the chops on a dish and pour over the reduced juices. Garnish with parsley.

Menu Suggestion
Serve with jacket potatoes and broccoli.

STIR-FRIED CHICKEN WITH VEGETABLES AND CASHEW NUTS

0.40	335 cals

Serves 4

1 bunch spring onions

3 celery sticks

1 green pepper

100 g (4 oz) cauliflower florets

2 carrots

175 g (6 oz) button mushrooms

4 boneless chicken breasts

30 ml (2 tbsp) sesame or vegetable oil

10 ml (2 tsp) cornflour

30 ml (2 tbsp) dry sherry

15 ml (1 tbsp) soy sauce

15 ml (1 tbsp) hoisin sauce (see box)

5 ml (1 tsp) soft brown sugar

150 ml ($\frac{1}{4}$ pint) water

75 g (3 oz) unsalted cashew nuts

salt and freshly ground pepper

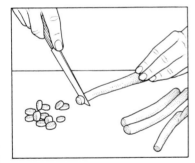

1 Prepare the vegetables. Trim the spring onions and slice them into thin rings. Trim the celery and slice finely.

2 Halve the green pepper, remove the core and seeds and slice the flesh into thin strips. Divide the cauliflower florets into tiny sprigs.

3 Peel the carrots, then grate into thin slivers using the coarse side of a conical or box grater or cut into matchsticks. Wipe the mushrooms and slice them finely.

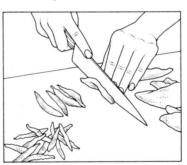

4 Skin the chicken and cut into bite-sized strips about 4 cm (1$\frac{1}{2}$ inches) long with a sharp knife.

5 Heat the oil in a wok or deep frying pan, add the prepared vegetables and stir-fry over brisk heat for 3 minutes. Remove with a slotted spoon and set aside.

6 In a jug, mix the cornflour to a paste with the sherry, soy sauce and hoisin sauce, then add the sugar and water.

7 Add the chicken strips to the pan and stir-fry over moderate heat until lightly coloured on all sides. Pour the cornflour mixture into the pan and bring to the boil, stirring constantly until thickened.

8 Return the vegetables to the pan. Add the cashew nuts and seasoning to taste, and stir-fry for a few minutes more. Serve immediately.

Menu Suggestion
With meat and vegetables cooked together, this Chinese-style dish is quite substantial. Serve with small bowls of rice—and chopsticks! Provide extra soy sauce for those who like it.

STIR-FRIED CHICKEN WITH VEGETABLES AND CASHEW NUTS

The hoisin sauce used in this Chinese-style recipe is just one of the many bottled and canned sauces which are used frequently in Chinese cookery. Look for them in oriental specialist shops and some large supermarkets — they will give an 'authentic' touch to your oriental dishes.

Chinese cooks use commercial sauces all the time. Hoisin sauce is made from soya bean flour, sugar, spices and food colouring; it is thick and pungent, a reddish-brown in colour. Add it to any stir-fried dish for extra body and flavour, and use it in sweet and sour dishes.

Marinated Chicken with Peanut Sauce

| 1.15* | ✳* | 685 cals |

* plus 24 hours marinating; freeze in the marinade

Serves 4

4 large chicken pieces

75 ml (5 tbsp) soy sauce

30 ml (2 tbsp) sesame or vegetable oil

30 ml (2 tbsp) clear honey

juice of 1 lemon

2.5 ml ($\frac{1}{2}$ tsp) chilli powder

1 red pepper

1 green pepper

75 g (3 oz) creamed coconut

75 ml (5 tbsp) dark crunchy peanut butter

10 ml (2 tsp) dark soft brown sugar

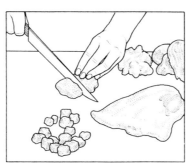

1 Skin the chicken pieces. Cut away the flesh from the bones with a sharp, pointed knife and slice the flesh into small cubes.

2 Put 45 ml (3 tbsp) of the soy sauce in a bowl with the oil, honey, lemon juice and chilli powder. Whisk with a fork until well combined.

3 Add the cubes of chicken to the marinade, stir well to coat, then cover and leave to marinate for 24 hours. Turn the chicken occasionally during this time.

4 When ready to cook, cut the red and green peppers in half, remove the cores and seeds and cut the flesh into neat squares.

5 Thread the chicken cubes and pepper squares on 4 oiled kebab skewers, place on a rack in the grill pan and brush liberally with the marinade.

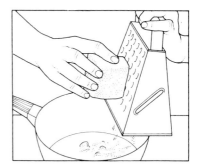

6 To make the peanut sauce. Grate the creamed coconut into a heavy-based saucepan. Add 150 ml ($\frac{1}{4}$ pint) boiling water and bring slowly back to the boil, stirring constantly. Simmer, stirring, until the coconut has dissolved.

7 Add the peanut butter, remaining soy sauce and the sugar to the pan and whisk to combine. Simmer very gently over the lowest possible heat, stirring occasionally until smooth.

8 Meanwhile, grill the chicken under moderate heat for 15 minutes, turning the skewers frequently and brushing with the remaining marinade. Serve hot.

Menu Suggestion
Serve the kebabs on a bed of brown rice or noodles, with a little of the sauce poured over. Hand the remaining sauce separately in a bowl. A cool, crisp salad of cucumber strips, spring onions and beansprouts tossed in oil, lemon juice and seasoning would make a refreshing follow-up to this dish.

CHICKEN AND SPINACH PIE WITH MUSHROOMS

| 1.10 | ✳* | 538 cals |

* freeze at step 6, before baking

Serves 4

4 cooked chicken portions

900 g (2 lb) fresh spinach or 450 g (1 lb) frozen leaf spinach

1.25 ml ($\frac{1}{4}$ tsp) grated nutmeg

salt and freshly ground pepper

568 ml (1 pint) milk

45 ml (3 tbsp) wholewheat flour

5 ml (1 tsp) dried tarragon

225 g (8 oz) button mushrooms, wiped and roughly chopped

1 egg, beaten

50 g (2 oz) Gruyère cheese

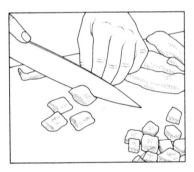

1 Skin the chicken portions and then remove the meat from the bones. Cut the meat into bite-sized pieces.

2 Trim the fresh spinach, discarding any thick stalks. Wash the leaves thoroughly, then place in a saucepan with only the water that clings to them. Cover the pan and cook for about 5 minutes until tender. Drain and chop roughly. If using frozen spinach, put in a heavy-based saucepan and heat gently for 7–10 minutes until defrosted. Season the spinach with the nutmeg and plenty of salt and freshly ground pepper.

3 Put the milk and flour in a blender or food processor. Blend until evenly mixed, then pour into a heavy-based saucepan. Bring slowly to boiling point, then simmer for 5 minutes, stirring frequently, until thickened.

4 Remove the sauce from the heat, reserve one third and stir the chicken, tarragon and seasoning to taste into the remaining sauce.

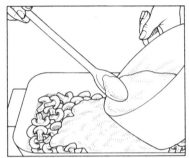

5 Spread one-third of the spinach over the bottom of a lightly greased ovenproof dish. Arrange half of the mushrooms on top of the spinach then pour over half of the chicken sauce. Repeat these layers once more, then spread over the remaining spinach.

6 Stir the egg into the reserved sauce, then pour over the spinach. Grate the cheese over the top. Bake in the oven at 190°C (375°F) mark 5 for about 30 minutes or until the topping is bubbling. Serve hot.

Menu Suggestion
Serve with creamed potatoes and braised leeks.

TURKEY ESCALOPES EN PAPILLOTE

| 1.00 | £ £ | 230–260 cals |

Serves 4

4 turkey breasts, total weight 550–700 g ($1\frac{1}{4}$–$1\frac{1}{2}$ lb), boned

15 ml (1 tbsp) corn oil

1 small red pepper, cored, seeded and thinly sliced

225 g (8 oz) tomatoes, skinned and sliced

30 ml (2 tbsp) chopped fresh parsley

salt and freshly ground pepper

60 ml (4 tbsp) medium dry sherry

40 g ($1\frac{1}{2}$ oz) fresh wholewheat breadcrumbs, toasted

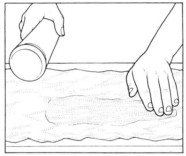

1 Split each turkey breast through its thickness with a sharp knife, then bat out between 2 sheets of greaseproof paper to make 8 thin escalopes.

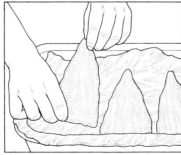

2 Place a large sheet of foil on a baking sheet and brush lightly with the oil. Put half of the turkey escalopes side by side on the foil.

3 Blanch the pepper slices for 1 minute in boiling water, drain and refresh under cold running water. Pat dry with absorbent kitchen paper.

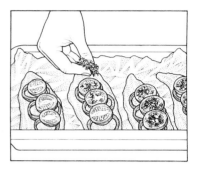

4 Layer the pepper and tomato slices on top of the escalopes with half of the parsley and seasoning to taste.

5 Cover with the remaining escalopes, spoon 15 ml (1 tbsp) sherry over each and close up the foil like a parcel.

6 Bake in the oven at 180°C (350°F) mark 4 for 35–40 minutes or until the meat is tender when pierced with a fork or skewer.

7 Arrange the escalopes on a warmed serving dish, cover and keep warm in the oven turned to its lowest setting. Transfer the juices to a pan and reduce to 60 ml (4 tbsp), then spoon over the turkey. Sprinkle with the freshly toasted breadcrumbs and the remaining parsley and serve immediately.

Menu Suggestion
A good choice for entertaining, serve Turkey Escalopes en Papillote with new potatoes and tiny fresh green peas.

KIDNEYS PROVENÇAL

| 0.35 | 211 cals |

Serves 4

12–16 lambs' kidneys

30 ml (2 tbsp) olive oil

1 large onion, skinned and
   chopped

1–2 garlic cloves, skinned and
   crushed

3 medium courgettes, trimmed
   and sliced

4 large tomatoes, skinned and
   roughly chopped

100 ml (4 fl oz) red wine or stock

10 ml (2 tsp) chopped fresh basil
   or 5 ml (1 tsp) dried basil

salt and freshly ground pepper

12 black olives

sprigs of chervil, to garnish

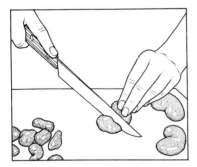

1 Skin the kidneys, then cut
each one in half. Snip out the
cores with kitchen scissors. Cut
each half into two.

2 Heat the oil in a large heavy-
based frying pan, add the onion
and garlic to the pan and fry
gently for 5 minutes until soft but
not coloured.

3 Add the kidneys and fry over
low heat for 3 minutes until
they change colour. Shake the pan
and toss the kidneys frequently
during frying.

4 Add the courgettes, tomatoes
and wine or stock and bring to
the boil, stirring constantly. Lower
the heat and add half the basil
with seasoning to taste. Simmer
gently for 8 minutes until the
kidneys are tender.

5 Add the olives to the pan and
heat through for 1–2
minutes. Taste and adjust the
seasoning. Sprinkle with the
remaining basil and chervil just
before serving. Serve very hot.

Menu Suggestion
This strongly flavoured dish needs
a contrasting bland accompaniment such as plain boiled rice.
Follow with a simple green salad,
cheese and fresh fruit for a
complete, well-balanced meal.

LIVER WITH VERMOUTH

0.35	£	319 cals

Serves 4

450 g (1 lb) lamb's liver, sliced

15 ml (1 tbsp) wholewheat flour

30 ml (2 tbsp) vegetable oil

1 onion, skinned and chopped

1 garlic clove, skinned and crushed

finely grated rind and juice of 1 orange

finely grated rind and juice of 1 lemon

60 ml (4 tbsp) sweet vermouth or sherry

30 ml (2 tbsp) chopped fresh parsley

salt and freshly ground pepper

few orange and lemon slices, to garnish

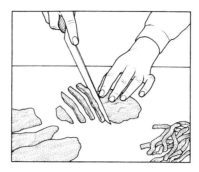

1 Cut the liver into thin strips, trimming away all ducts and gristle. Coat in the flour.

2 Heat the oil in a flameproof casserole, add the onion and garlic to the casserole and fry gently for 5 minutes until soft but not coloured.

3 Add the liver strips and cook over high heat until browned on all sides.

4 Add the orange and lemon rind and juices and the vermouth and bring to the boil. Stir constantly with a wooden spoon to scrape up any sediment and juices from the base of the casserole, and continue boiling until the sauce reduces.

5 Lower the heat and add half the parsley and salt and freshly ground pepper to taste.

6 Dip the orange and lemon slices in the remaining chopped parsley. Transfer the liver and sauce to a warmed serving dish. Garnish with the orange and lemon slices and serve immediately, while piping hot.

Menu Suggestion
Serve this tangy liver dish on a bed of brown rice or with wholewheat noodles. Stir-fried beansprouts, mushrooms or spinach would make a good vegetable accompaniment.

TANDOORI FISH

| 0.45 | 95 cals |

Serves 2

225 g (8 oz) thick white fish fillet
   (monkfish, cod, haddock)

30 ml (2 tbsp) natural yogurt

15 ml (1 tbsp) lemon juice

1 small garlic clove, skinned and
   crushed

1.25 ml ($\frac{1}{4}$ tsp) ground coriander

1.25 ml ($\frac{1}{4}$ tsp) ground cumin

1.25 ml ($\frac{1}{4}$ tsp) ground turmeric

pinch of paprika

margarine or butter

fresh coriander and lime wedges,
   to garnish

1 Skin the fish fillet, and then
   cut into 2 equal portions
with a sharp knife.

2 Make the tandoori marinade.
   Put the yogurt and lemon juice
in a bowl with the garlic and
spices. Stir well to mix.

3 Place the fish on a sheet of
   foil and brush with the
marinade. Leave in a cool place for
30 minutes.

4 Dot the fish with a few knobs
   of margarine or butter. Cook
under a preheated moderate grill
for about 8 minutes, turning
frequently. Serve immediately,
garnished with fresh coriander and
lime wedges.

Menu Suggestion
Serve on a bed of saffron rice,
accompanied by a green salad with
plenty of chopped fresh coriander.

TANDOORI FISH

This recipe is given its name
from the special clay *tandoor*
oven which is used for cooking
in India. Meat, poultry and fish
are marinated in a yogurt and
spice mixture to tenderise and
add flavour, then cooked in the
tandoor. It is the combination of
the marinade and the searing
temperatures of the charcoal-
fired clay oven which gives such
a spectacular colour and
delicious taste. Small tandoori
oven sets are available at
specialist kitchen shops and
departments, but these must be
used outside for adequate
ventilation and safety reasons.
Obviously they cannot in any way
compare with the real thing in
size or intensity of heat, but if
you like the flavour of tandoori
food it is worth considering
buying one as an alternative to
cooking on a barbecue in
summertime.

FISH KEBABS

0.20*	187 cals

* plus 2 hours marinating

Serves 4

700 g (1½ lb) monkfish fillets,
skinned

60 ml (4 tbsp) sunflower oil

juice of 2 limes or 1 lemon

1 small onion, skinned and roughly
chopped

2 garlic cloves, skinned and
crushed

2.5 ml (½ tsp) fennel seed

2.5 ml (½ tsp) dried thyme

freshly ground pepper

1 green pepper, halved, cored and
seeded

16 whole cherry tomatoes or
4 small tomatoes, quartered

8 bay leaves

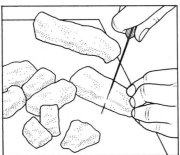

1 Cut the monkfish into 4 cm
(1½ inch) chunks. Place the oil,
lime or lemon juice, onion, garlic,
fennel, thyme and pepper in a
blender or food processor and
blend until smooth. Toss the fish
in this mixture, cover and
marinate for at least 2 hours.

2 Meanwhile, place the green
pepper in a saucepan of cold
water and bring to the boil. Drain
and cut into 12 pieces.

3 Thread the fish, green pepper,
tomatoes and bay leaves on to
4 oiled skewers. Reserve the
marinade for basting.

4 Cook the kebabs under a preheated moderate grill for about
10 minutes, basting with the
marinade and turning once.

Menu Suggestion
Serve with steamed brown rice
and a fennel salad to complement
the flavour of the marinade.

FISH KEBABS
In summertime, these kebabs
would be excellent cooked on the
barbecue—the additional flavour
of the charcoal goes well with
quick-cooking fish, and they
would make an unusual
alternative to steaks, chicken and
chops. Follow the recipe exactly
as above and make sure the
barbecue coals are hot before
cooking—they should look grey
in daylight, glowing red at night.
Food, especially delicately
textured fish, should never be
put over coals that are flaming,
so wait for all flames to die down
before starting to cook. Oil the
barbecue grid well before placing
the kebabs over the fire.

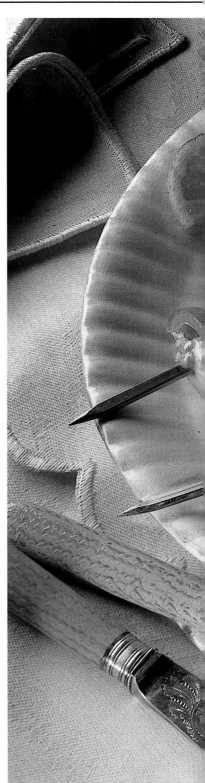

STUFFED PLAICE FILLETS WITH MUSHROOM SAUCE

| 1.10 | 🍴 | 185 cals |

Serves 4

4 double plaice fillets

salt and freshly ground pepper

225 g (8 oz) cottage cheese with prawns (see box)

1.25 ml (¼ tsp) Tabasco sauce, or less according to taste

finely grated rind and juice of 1 lemon

225 g (8 oz) button mushrooms, wiped and thinly sliced

90 ml (6 tbsp) dry white wine

5 ml (1 tsp) chopped fresh tarragon or dill or 2.5 ml (½ tsp) dried

8 unshelled prawns and fresh tarragon or dill sprigs, to garnish

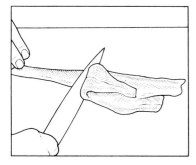

1 Skin the plaice fillets. Lay them flat, skin side down, on a board or work surface. Dip your fingers in salt and grip the tail end, then separate the flesh from the skin at this point with a sharp knife. Work the knife slowly between the skin and flesh using a sawing action until the opposite end of the fillet is reached. Cut each fillet into two lengthways.

2 Drain off any liquid from the cottage cheese, then mash the cheese with half of the Tabasco sauce, the grated lemon rind and seasoning to taste.

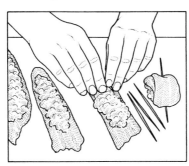

3 Lay the plaice fillets flat, with their skinned side facing upwards. Divide the cheese filling equally between them, then roll up and secure with wooden cocktail sticks, if necessary.

4 Place the stuffed fish rolls close together in a single layer in a lightly oiled ovenproof dish. Sprinkle the mushrooms around the fish, then pour over the wine mixed with the lemon juice and remaining Tabasco. Sprinkle with seasoning to taste.

5 Cover the dish with foil and cook in the oven at 180°C (350°F) mark 4 for 20 minutes or until the fish is just tender.

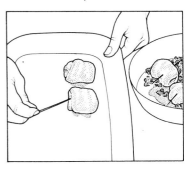

6 Remove the rolls from the liquid and discard the cocktail sticks. Arrange the fish on a warmed serving dish, cover loosely with foil and keep warm in the oven turned to its lowest setting.

7 Put the cooked mushrooms in a blender or food processor. Add the tarragon or dill and blend until smooth. Pour into a pan and heat through. Taste and adjust seasoning.

8 Pour a little sauce over each plaice roll, then top with a prawn and a tarragon or dill sprig. Serve immediately, with any remaining sauce handed separately in a jug.

Menu Suggestion
Serve this low calorie dish with jacket-baked potatoes or potatoes boiled in their skins, and a seasonal green vegetable or a watercress and chicory salad.

STUFFED PLAICE FILLETS WITH MUSHROOM SAUCE

The cottage cheese with prawns used in the stuffing for these plaice fillets is available in cartons from selected super-markets. Look for a good-quality brand which is thick and firm-textured. Some brands of cottage cheese are watery and will not be suitable for this dish. If there is a little water on the surface of the cheese when you open the carton, be sure to drain it off before use.

MACKEREL PARCELS

1.00	£	319 cals

Serves 4

**4 fresh mackerel, weighing about
    175 g (6 oz) each**

**about 25 g (1 oz) margarine or
    butter**

½ large cucumber

60 ml (4 tbsp) white wine vinegar

30 ml (2 tbsp) chopped fresh mint

5 ml (1 tsp) sugar

salt and freshly ground pepper

**natural yogurt and chopped fresh
    mint, to serve**

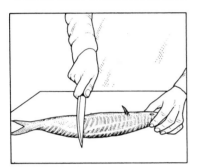

1 With the back of a knife and
working from the tail towards
the head, scrape off the scales
from the skin of the mackerel.

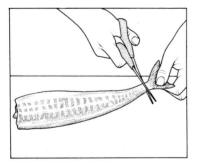

2 Cut off the heads just below
the gills with a sharp knife.
Cut off the fins and tails with
kitchen scissors.

3 Slit the underside of the fish
open from head to tail end
with a sharp knife or scissors.

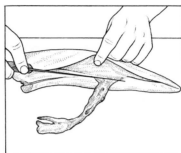

4 With the flat of the knife
blade, scrape out the entrails
of the fish, together with any
membranes and blood. Wash the
fish thoroughly inside and out
under cold running water.

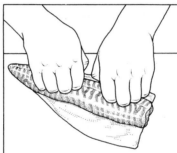

5 Lay the fish flat on a board or
work surface with the skin
uppermost. Press firmly along the
backbone with your knuckles (this
flattens the fish and loosens the
backbone).

6 Turn the fish over and lift out
the backbone with the help of
a knife. Cut each fish lengthways
into 2 fillets. Dry thoroughly with
absorbent kitchen paper.

7 Brush 8 squares of kitchen foil
with a little margarine. Put a
mackerel fillet in the centre of
each square, skin side down.

8 Arrange the cucumber slices
on one half of the mackerel
fillets, then sprinkle with the
vinegar, mint, sugar and seasoning
to taste. Dot with the remaining
margarine in tiny pieces.

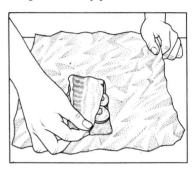

9 Fold the mackerel fillets over
to enclose the cucumber filling, then wrap in the foil. Place
the foil parcels in a single layer in
an ovenproof dish. Cook in the
oven at 200°C (400°F) mark 6 for
30 minutes until the fish is tender.

10 To serve, unwrap the foil
parcels and carefully place
the mackerel fillets in a circle on a
warmed platter. Spoon yogurt in
the centre and sprinkle with mint.

Menu Suggestion
Serve hot with potatoes boiled in
their jackets, or serve cold with a
potato salad.

MACKEREL PARCELS
Fresh mackerel, like herring, are
an inexpensive yet much
neglected fish. And yet they are a
good source of first-class protein,
plus the minerals calcium and
phosphorus which are essential
for healthy bones. Mackerel flesh
is also rich in vitamins A and D,
so it makes sense to include it
regularly in a healthy diet.
Always make sure to cook
mackerel on the day of purchase
as it quickly deteriorates after
catching.

FISHERMAN'S PIE

1.00	£	406 cals

Serves 4

65 g (2½ oz) margarine or butter

100 g (4 oz) red pepper, cored,
   seeded and thinly sliced

100 g (4 oz) green pepper, cored,
   seeded and thinly sliced

50 g (2 oz) onion, skinned and sliced

salt and freshly ground pepper

100 g (4 oz) button mushrooms,
   wiped and halved

450 ml (¾ pint) tomato juice

550 g (1¼ lb) cod fillet, skinned

450 g (1 lb) potatoes, peeled and
   thinly sliced

50 g (2 oz) Edam cheese, grated

1 Melt 25 g (1 oz) of the margarine in a frying pan, add the peppers and onion and fry gently for 10 minutes until soft but not coloured. Transfer to a 2.3 litre (4 pint) ovenproof dish. Season well.

2 Cook the mushrooms in the remaining fat in the frying pan, stirring frequently, for 3–4 minutes until evenly coloured.

3 Pour the tomato juice evenly over the pepper and onion mixture in the dish.

4 Cut the fish into large cubes. Arrange the cubes on top of the tomato juice, pressing them down gently into the juice. Top with the mushrooms. Season again with salt and pepper.

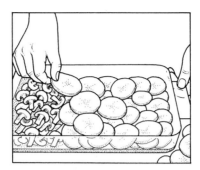

5 Arrange the sliced potatoes on top of the mushrooms. Melt the remaining margarine and brush over the potatoes. Bake in the oven at 190°C (375°F) mark 5 for 25 minutes.

6 Sprinkle the grated cheese over the pie, return to the oven and bake for a further 15 minutes until melted and bubbling. Serve hot, straight from the dish.

Menu Suggestion
Try Fisherman's Pie with fresh spinach. Wash the spinach and cook for a few minutes in the water clinging to the leaves, then drain, roughly chop and lightly season with salt, pepper and freshly grated nutmeg.

FISHERMAN'S PIE
It is important to slice the potatoes thinly for the topping on this pie or they will not cook through in the time stated. The best way to slice raw potatoes really thinly is to use a mandolin slicer. These are invaluable for many potato dishes, especially the French *gratin dauphinois* in which thinly sliced potatoes are cooked with cream and cheese. To be absolutely sure of tender potatoes for this Fisherman's Pie, you can parboil them first for 10 minutes. Drain them thoroughly afterwards, leave until cool enough to handle, then slice.

Vegetarian Main Dishes

Main courses without meat, poultry or fish are not reserved for vegetarians—they are satisfying and nutritious for everyone. The recipes in this chapter illustrate just how interesting, varied and colourful main dishes can be without a central theme of meat or fish. If served with plenty of fresh fruit and vegetables, plus grains, nuts and cereals, these dishes can form the basis of a well-balanced and highly nutritious vegetarian diet, although they are not suitable for vegans, as they do contain milk, cheese and eggs.

STUFFED BAKED AUBERGINES

| 1.00 | £ | 184 cals |

Serves 4

2 aubergines

25 g (1 oz) margarine or butter

4 small tomatoes, skinned and chopped

10 ml (2 tsp) chopped fresh marjoram or 5 ml (1 tsp) dried

1 shallot, skinned and chopped

1 onion, skinned and chopped

50 g (2 oz) brown breadcrumbs

salt and freshly ground pepper

50 g (2 oz) cheese, grated

parsley sprigs, to garnish

1 Steam (see page 149) or boil the whole aubergines for about 30 minutes until tender.

2 Cut the aubergines in half lengthways, scoop out the flesh and chop finely. Reserve the aubergine shells.

3 Melt the margarine in a pan, add the tomatoes, marjoram, shallot and onion and cook gently for 10 minutes. Stir in the aubergine flesh and a few breadcrumbs, then add salt and freshly ground pepper to taste.

4 Stuff the aubergine shells with this mixture, sprinkle with the remaining breadcrumbs and then with the grated cheese. Place in a grill pan and grill until golden brown on top. Serve hot, garnished with parsley sprigs.

Menu Suggestion
Serve with brown rice and follow with a cucumber and watercress salad.

STUFFED BAKED AUBERGINES

This recipe can also be used for courgettes. Allow 2–3 medium-sized courgettes per person. Cut them in half lengthways and carefully scoop out the flesh with a sharp-edged teaspoon. Blanch in boiling salted water for 4 minutes only, then drain thoroughly. Chop the scooped-out raw courgette flesh and cook for 10 minutes with the tomato mixture. Stand the courgette halves side by side (so that they stand upright) in a well-buttered baking tin before stuffing and grilling. For a more substantial main course dish, make a separate cheese sauce and serve with the stuffed courgettes so that people can help themselves. The flavour of Greek Feta cheese goes well with courgettes and aubergines and can also be used with the breadcrumbs for the topping.

VEGETABLE LASAGNE

1.10	£	460 cals

Serves 4

175 g (6 oz) lasagne verde

salt and freshly ground pepper

30 ml (2 tbsp) vegetable oil

2 medium onions, skinned and thinly sliced

350 g (12 oz) tomatoes, skinned and thinly sliced

350 g (12 oz) courgettes, trimmed and thinly sliced

15 ml (1 tbsp) tomato purée

5 ml (1 tsp) chopped fresh basil or 2.5 ml ($\frac{1}{2}$ tsp) dried

25 g (1 oz) walnut pieces, chopped

450 ml ($\frac{3}{4}$ pint) natural yogurt

2 eggs

75 g (3 oz) Cheddar cheese, grated

1.25 ml ($\frac{1}{4}$ tsp) ground cumin

a little vegetable oil, for brushing

1 Cook the lasagne in a large saucepan of boiling salted water with 15 ml (1 tbsp) oil for 15 minutes. Drain in single sheets on absorbent kitchen paper.

2 Heat the remaining oil in a pan, add the onion, tomatoes and 300 g (10 oz) of the courgettes and fry gently until the tomatoes begin to break down. Stir in the tomato purée, basil and plenty of seasoning.

3 Grease a deep-sided 2 litre (3$\frac{1}{2}$ pint) ovenproof dish. Layer the vegetables, lasagne and nuts in the dish, ending with a layer of lasagne.

4 Beat the yogurt and eggs together, then stir in the cheese, cumin and seasoning to taste. Pour over the lasagne.

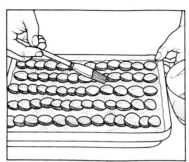

5 Arrange the remaining courgettes over the yogurt topping and brush them lightly with oil. Bake the lasagne in the oven at 200°C (400°F) mark 6 for about 40 minutes or until set. Serve hot, straight from the dish.

Menu Suggestion
Serve with crusty bread and a mixed green salad.

VEGETABLE LASAGNE
The lasagne verde used in this recipe is the green, spinach-flavoured lasagne. Most varieties must be pre-boiled before layering with the other ingredients in the dish, as indicated in the method here. To save time and trouble, look for the pre-cooked lasagne which can be placed straight in the dish from the packet without boiling. Most supermarkets and health food shops sell this type of lasagne, which comes in many different types, including wholewheat.

SPINACH ROULADE

| 1.10 | 🍴 🍴 ✳ | 182 cals |

Serves 4

900 g (2 lb) fresh spinach, washed and trimmed

4 eggs, size 2, separated

salt and freshly ground pepper

100 g (4 oz) curd cheese

30 ml (2 tbsp) natural yogurt

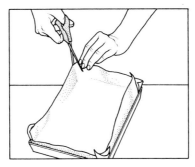

1 Grease and line a 35.5 × 25.5 cm (14 × 10 inch) Swiss roll tin. Set aside.

2 Chop the spinach coarsely. Place in a saucepan with only the water that clings to the leaves. Simmer for 5 minutes, drain.

3 Cool spinach slightly; beat in egg yolks and salt and freshly ground pepper to taste.

4 Whisk the egg whites until stiff, then fold into the spinach mixture, until evenly incorporated.

5 Spread the mixture in the tin. Bake at 200°C (400°F) mark 6 for 20 minutes until firm. Beat the cheese and yogurt together.

6 When the roulade is cooked, turn out on to a sheet of greaseproof paper, peel off the lining paper and spread immediately and quickly with the cheese mixture.

7 Roll up the roulade by gently lifting the greaseproof paper. Place, seam side down, on a serving platter. Serve hot or cold, cut into thick slices.

Menu Suggestion

Serve hot with new potatoes in their skins or cold with a minted potato salad. Follow with a tomato salad.

LEEK TART

1.20   ✳   524 cals

Serves 6

75 ml (5 tbsp) vegetable oil

225 g (8 oz) plain wholewheat flour, plus 30 ml (2 tbsp)

salt and freshly ground pepper

75 g (3 oz) margarine or butter

1.4 kg (3 lb) leeks, white parts only, sliced — 700 g ($1\frac{1}{2}$ lb) prepared weight

450 ml ($\frac{3}{4}$ pint) milk

pinch of grated nutmeg

2 eggs

75 g (3 oz) Gruyère cheese, grated

1 Make the pastry. Put the oil and 30 ml (2 tbsp) cold water in a bowl. Beat well with a fork to form an emulsion.

2 Mix the 225 g (8 oz) flour and a pinch of salt together. Gradually add to the oil mixture to make a dough.

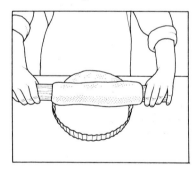

3 Roll out the dough on a floured surface or between pieces of greaseproof paper, and use to line a 25 cm (10 inch) flan tin or dish.

4 Prick the base, line with foil or greaseproof and baking beans and bake blind in the oven at 190°C (375°F) mark 5 for 10 minutes until set.

5 Meanwhile, melt 50 g (2 oz) of the margarine in a heavy saucepan, add the leeks, cover and sweat very gently, without allowing to colour, for 10 minutes. Add just enough water to stop the leeks from burning, shake the pan and cook until tender.

6 In a separate saucepan, melt the remaining margarine, stir in the 30 ml (2 tbsp) flour and cook for 1–2 minutes without allowing to brown. Gradually stir in the milk and cooking liquid from the leeks until smooth. Add the nutmeg and seasoning to taste and simmer for a few minutes, stirring continuously.

7 Spread the leeks out evenly in the pastry case. Beat the eggs and add to the white sauce with half the grated cheese. Pour over the leeks. Sprinkle with the remaining cheese.

8 Bake in the oven at 200°C (400°F) mark 6 for 25–30 minutes or until the top is slightly risen and golden brown.

Menu Suggestion
Serve with creamed potatoes and baked tomatoes.

ROOT VEGETABLE HOT POT

| 0.55 | £ | 120–180 cals |

Serves 4–6

1 onion

225 g (8 oz) potatoes

225 g (8 oz) swede

4 medium carrots

2 medium leeks

10 ml (2 tsp) yeast extract

salt and freshly ground pepper

300 ml (½ pint) vegetable stock

30 ml (2 tbsp) chopped fresh
   parsley

100 g (4 oz) mature Cheddar
   cheese, grated

1 Prepare the vegetables. Skin and finely chop the onion. Peel the potatoes and swede and cut into chunks. Peel the carrots and slice thinly.

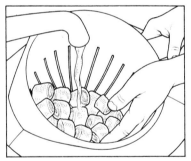

2 Trim the leeks, cut into thick rings, then place in a colander and rinse thoroughly under cold running water.

3 Put the prepared vegetables in a flameproof casserole with the yeast extract and seasoning to taste. Pour in the stock and bring to the boil, stirring to mix all the ingredients together.

4 Cover the casserole and simmer for 30 minutes until the vegetables are tender. Stir in the parsley, then taste and adjust the seasoning.

5 Sprinkle the cheese over the top of the vegetables, then put under a moderate grill for 5 minutes until melted and bubbling. Serve hot, straight from the casserole.

Menu Suggestion
Serve with chunky slices of wholemeal bread, or on a bed of boiled brown rice.

ROOT VEGETABLE HOT POT

To make this hot pot into a more substantial dish, why not make it in a pie dish and top with pastry? To do this, follow the recipe up to step 3, then put the prepared vegetables in a pie dish instead of the flameproof casserole. Stir in the parsley and top with the cheese. Make 175 g (6 oz) wholemeal pastry according to the recipe on page 157, then cut out to make a lid for the dish. Cut a thin strip of pastry to go around the rim of the dish, then stick on with water. Brush the strip of pastry with water, then place the lid on top. Make a hole in the centre and decorate with pastry trimmings if liked, and then glaze with beaten egg. Bake in the oven at 190°C (375°F) mark 5 for 30 minutes, covering the top of the pie with foil or greaseproof if it shows signs of overbrowning.

CAULIFLOWER AND COURGETTE BAKE

1.10	£	278 cals

Serves 4

700 g (1½ lb) cauliflower

salt and freshly ground pepper

50 g (2 oz) margarine or butter

225 g (8 oz) courgettes, trimmed and thinly sliced

45 ml (3 tbsp) wholewheat flour

150 ml (¼ pint) milk

3 eggs, separated

15 ml (1 tbsp) grated Parmesan cheese

1 Divide the cauliflower into small florets, trimming off thick stalks and leaves. Cook in boiling salted water for 10–12 minutes until tender.

2 Meanwhile, in a separate pan, melt 25 g (1 oz) of the margarine, add the courgettes and cook until beginning to soften. Remove from the pan with a slotted spoon and drain on absorbent kitchen paper.

3 Melt the remaining margarine in the pan, stir in the flour and cook, stirring, for 1–2 minutes. Remove from the heat and add the milk a little at a time, whisking constantly after each addition. Return to the heat and bring to the boil, stirring. Lower the heat and simmer until thickened.

4 Drain the cauliflower well and place in a blender or food processor with the warm sauce, egg yolks and plenty of seasoning. Blend together until evenly mixed, then turn into a large bowl.

5 Whisk the egg whites until stiff and carefully fold into the cauliflower mixture with a large metal spoon until they are evenly distributed.

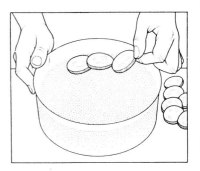

6 Spoon half of the mixture into a 1.6 litre (2¾ pint) soufflé dish. Arrange the courgettes on top, reserving a few for garnish, then cover with the remaining cauliflower mixture and reserved drained courgettes.

7 Sprinkle over the Parmesan cheese and bake in the oven at 190°C (375°F) mark 5 for 35–40 minutes or until golden. Serve.

Menu Suggestion

This vegetable soufflé mixture is best served with braised chicory or a mixed salad.

VEGETABLE BIRYANI

| 0.55 | 519 cals |

Serves 4

350 g (12 oz) Basmati rice (see box)

1.4 litres (2½ pints) water

salt and freshly ground pepper

50 g (2 oz) ghee or clarified butter
(see box)

1 large onion, skinned and chopped

2.5 cm (1 inch) piece fresh root
ginger, skinned and grated

1–2 garlic cloves, skinned and
crushed

5 ml (1 tsp) ground coriander

10 ml (2 tsp) ground cumin

5 ml (1 tsp) ground turmeric

2.5 ml (½ tsp) chilli powder

3 medium carrots, peeled and
thinly sliced

225 g (8 oz) fresh or frozen green
beans, trimmed and cut in 2
lengthways

225 g (8 oz) cauliflower florets,
divided into small sprigs

5 ml (1 tsp) garam masala

juice of 1 lemon

hard-boiled egg slices and
coriander sprigs, to garnish

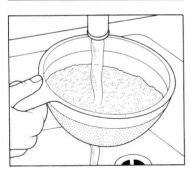

1 Put the rice in a sieve and hold
under cold running water until
the water runs clear.

2 Put the rice in a saucepan with
600 ml (1 pint) of the water
and 5 ml (1 tsp) salt. Bring to the
boil, then simmer for 10 minutes
until only just tender.

3 Meanwhile, melt the ghee in a
heavy-based large saucepan,
add the onion, ginger and garlic
and fry gently for 5 minutes until
soft but not coloured. Add the
coriander, cumin, turmeric and
chilli powder and fry for 2
minutes more, stirring constantly
to avoid catching and burning.

4 Remove the rice from the heat
and drain. Add the remaining
water to the onion and spice mixture with seasoning to taste. Stir
well and bring to the boil. Add the
carrots and beans and simmer for
15 minutes, then add the
cauliflower and simmer for a
further 10 minutes. Lastly, add
the rice. Fold gently to mix and
simmer until reheated.

5 Stir the garam masala and
lemon juice into the biryani
and simmer for a few minutes
more to reheat and allow the
flavours to develop. Taste and
adjust the seasoning, then turn
into a warmed serving dish.
Garnish with egg slices and
coriander and serve immediately.

Menu Suggestion
Serve this spicy dish with natural
yogurt (raita) for a refreshing
contrast, and a salad of sliced
tomatoes, onions, cucumber and
peppers dressed with oil,
coriander, ginger and chilli
powder to taste.

VEGETABLE BIRYANI
Indian basmati rice is expensive,
but worth buying for its unique
flavour and fluffy texture. Look
for it in Indian shops and
specialist supermarkets. Rinse or
soak it before cooking, to remove
excess starch.
    Ghee is the Indian word for
clarified butter. It is used in
cooking because it can be heated
to high temperatures without
burning. Buy it at Indian shops,
or clarify butter yourself.

MOONG DAL AND SPINACH

| 0.40* | £ | 279 cals |

* plus 2 hours soaking

Serves 6

225 g (8 oz) moong dal (split,
   washed moong beans—see box)

900 g (2 lb) fresh spinach, washed
   and trimmed, or 450 g (1 lb)
   chopped frozen spinach

75 g (3 oz) ghee or clarified butter
   (see box on page 102)

100 g (4 oz) onion, skinned and
   finely chopped

15 g ($\frac{1}{2}$ oz) fresh root ginger, peeled
   and finely chopped

1 garlic clove, skinned and crushed

10 ml (2 tsp) ground coriander

5 ml (1 tsp) ground turmeric

2.5 ml ($\frac{1}{2}$ tsp) chilli powder

1.25 ml ($\frac{1}{4}$ tsp) asafoetida
   (optional—see box)

300 ml ($\frac{1}{2}$ pint) water

salt and freshly ground pepper

lemon wedges, to garnish

1 Rinse the dal under cold
running water. Place in a bowl,
cover with cold water and leave to
soak for about 2 hours. Drain.

2 Place the fresh spinach in a
saucepan with only the water
that clings to the leaves. Cover and
cook gently for about 5 minutes
until tender. Drain well and chop
roughly. If using frozen spinach,
place in a saucepan and cook for
7–10 minutes to remove as much
liquid as possible.

3 Melt the ghee in a large sauté
pan, add the onion, ginger and
garlic and fry gently for 2–3
minutes until lightly coloured.

4 Stir in the coriander, turmeric,
chilli powder, asafoetida, if
using, and the dal. Fry, stirring,
for 2–3 minutes.

5 Pour in the water, add seasoning to taste and bring to the
boil. Cover and simmer for about
15 minutes or until the dal is
almost tender. Add a little more
water if necessary, but the mixture
should be almost dry.

6 Stir in the spinach and cook,
stirring, for 2–3 minutes or
until heated through. Taste and
adjust the seasoning before
serving, garnished with lemon
wedges.

Menu Suggestion
Serve with warm wholemeal
chappattis (see page 156) and a
natural yogurt and cucumber
salad.

MOONG DAL AND SPINACH

The Indian word *dal* means
pulse. There are hundreds of
different kinds used in Indian
cookery—go to an Indian
specialist store or health food
shop for the best choice. There
are three types of *moong dal*
available, all of which are
extremely nutritious, with a high
vitamin A content. *Sabaat moong*
are whole mung beans, sprouted
to make beansprouts. *Moong dal*
chilke wali are split mung beans
without skins. The beans in this
recipe are *dhooli hui moong dal*—
split mung beans without skins,
pale yellow in colour.

   Asafoetida is a powder derived
from resin. It is often used with
pulses in Indian cookery, to
counteract flatulence. Buy it at
Indian shops, and only use it in
the minute quantity stated.

CRUNCHY WINTER SALAD

| 0.15 | £ | 512 cals |

Serves 4

2 dessert apples

finely grated rind and juice of $\frac{1}{2}$ lemon

45 ml (3 tbsp) sunflower oil

150 ml ($\frac{1}{4}$ pint) natural yogurt

salt and freshly ground pepper

225 g (8 oz) red cabbage, trimmed and finely sliced

1 small onion, skinned and finely sliced

2 celery sticks, trimmed and sliced

100 g (4 oz) Cheddar cheese, diced

100 g (4 oz) natural (unsalted) peanuts

grapefruit segments and celery leaves, to garnish

1 Quarter and core the apples, then cut into chunks. Toss in 30 ml (2 tbsp) lemon juice.

2 Make the dressing. In a bowl, whisk the remaining lemon juice with the rind, sunflower oil, yogurt and seasoning to taste until well emulsified.

3 Put the cabbage, onion, celery, apple, cheese and peanuts in a large bowl, pour over the dressing and toss well. Adjust seasoning. Garnish with the grapefruit segments and celery leaves.

Menu Suggestion
Accompany this salad with warm wholewheat rolls.

WHOLEWHEAT BRAZIL SALAD

$\boxed{1.45*}$ £ $\boxed{356–533 \text{ cals}}$

* plus overnight soaking and 30 minutes cooling

Serves 4–6

75 g (3 oz) dried black-eyed beans, soaked in cold water overnight

100 g (4 oz) wholewheat grain, soaked in cold water overnight

90 ml (6 tbsp) natural yogurt

30 ml (2 tbsp) olive oil

45 ml (3 tbsp) lemon juice

45 ml (3 tbsp) chopped fresh mint

salt and freshly ground pepper

½ cucumber, diced

225 g (8 oz) tomatoes, skinned and roughly chopped

100 g (4 oz) Cheddar cheese, grated

100 g (4 oz) Brazil nuts, roughly chopped

lettuce leaves and mint sprigs, to garnish

1 Drain the beans and place in a saucepan of water. Bring to the boil and simmer gently for 1½ hours or until tender.

2 Meanwhile, drain the wholewheat and place in a saucepan of water. Bring to the boil and simmer gently for 20–25 minutes or until tender. Drain, rinse well with cold water and cool for 30 minutes. When the beans are cooked, drain and cool for 30 minutes.

3 Whisk the yogurt and olive oil together with the lemon juice, mint and seasoning to taste.

4 Put the wholewheat, beans, cucumber, tomatoes, cheese and Brazil nuts in a bowl. Pour over the dressing and mix well.

5 Line a salad bowl with lettuce leaves and pile the wholewheat salad on top. Garnish and chill.

Menu Suggestion
Serve with crusty brown bread.

SPINACH AND MUSHROOM SALAD

| 0.30 | £ | 366 cals |

Serves 6

225 g (8 oz) fresh spinach, washed and trimmed

2 large slices of wholewheat bread

vegetable oil, for frying

2 oranges

10 ml (2 tsp) wholegrain mustard

1 garlic clove, skinned and crushed (optional)

90 ml (6 tbsp) sunflower oil

30 ml (2 tbsp) lemon juice

salt and freshly ground pepper

2 avocados

225 g (8 oz) button mushrooms, wiped and sliced

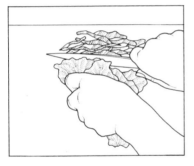

1 Shred the spinach leaves into small strips and place in a bowl. Set aside.

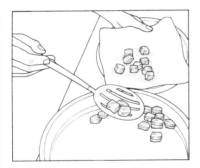

2 Make the croûtons. Cut the crusts off the slices of bread, then cut the bread into 5 mm (¼ inch) cubes or into shapes with a small cutter. Pour enough oil into a frying pan to just cover the base, add the bread cubes and fry over moderate heat until evenly browned. Drain.

3 Peel the oranges using a serrated knife, cutting away all the skin and pith. Cut the oranges into segments, removing the membrane. Discard any pips.

4 Whisk together the mustard, garlic, sunflower oil, lemon juice and seasoning to taste until well emulsified.

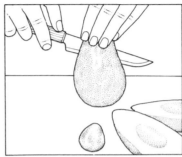

5 Halve the avocados and remove the stones. Peel the avocados and chop the flesh into even-sized chunks.

6 Place the oranges, avocados and mushrooms on top of the spinach and pour over the dressing. Mix together carefully and sprinkle with the croûtons. Serve immediately.

Menu Suggestion

Serve with baked potatoes for an easy main course dish.

BEAN, CHEESE AND AVOCADO SALAD

| 2.15* | 613 cals |

* plus overnight soaking

Serves 4

225 g (8 oz) dried red kidney beans, soaked in cold water overnight

90 ml (6 tbsp) olive oil

finely grated rind and juice of 1 lemon

1.25 ml ($\frac{1}{4}$ tsp) Tabasco sauce

salt and freshly ground pepper

175 g (6 oz) Edam cheese, rinded and diced

1 small onion, skinned and finely chopped

2 celery sticks, trimmed and finely chopped

2 tomatoes, skinned and chopped

1 ripe avocado

celery leaves, to garnish

1 Drain the kidney beans and rinse under cold running water. Put in a saucepan, cover with fresh cold water and bring to the boil. Boil rapidly for 10 minutes, then simmer for 1–1$\frac{1}{2}$ hours until tender.

2 Drain the beans and put in a bowl. Add the oil, lemon rind and juice, Tabasco and seasoning. Toss well, then leave until cold.

3 Add the cheese, onion, celery and tomatoes to the beans and toss again to mix the ingredients together. Cover and chill in the refrigerator until serving time.

4 When ready to serve, peel the avocado, cut in half and remove the stone. Chop the flesh into chunky pieces. Fold the avocado pieces gently into the bean salad and taste and adjust the seasoning. Garnish and serve.

Menu Suggestion
Serve with hot wholemeal rolls or jacket-baked potatoes.

BROWN RICE RING

0.45* £ 382 cals

* plus 1 hour chilling

Serves 4

225 g (8 oz) long grain brown rice

salt and freshly ground pepper

30 ml (2 tbsp) sunflower oil

juice of 1 lemon

30 ml (2 tbsp) wholegrain mustard

2 celery sticks, trimmed and
    finely chopped

225 g (8 oz) button mushrooms,
    wiped and finely sliced

100 g (4 oz) hazelnuts, roughly
    chopped

30 ml (2 tbsp) chopped mixed
    fresh herbs (parsley, marjoram,
    mint, basil, coriander)

watercress sprigs or orange and
    lemon slices, to garnish

1 Cook the rice in a large saucepan of boiling salted water for
about 30 minutes (or according to
packet instructions) until tender.
Drain thoroughly.

2 Tip the hot rice into a bowl.
Mix together the oil, lemon
juice, mustard and fork through
the rice. Add the celery, mushrooms
and nuts, then the herbs and
seasoning to taste. Fork through
again.

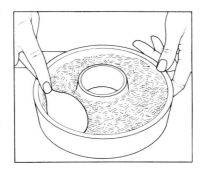

3 Spoon the rice mixture into a
lightly oiled 750 ml (1¼ pint)
ring mould, pressing it down
firmly so that the ingredients cling
together. Chill in the refrigerator
for at least 1 hour.

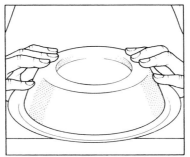

4 To serve. Place a serving plate
on top of the ring mould and
invert them so that the rice ring
turns out upside down on to the
plate. Fill the centre with watercress. Serve at room temperature.

Menu Suggestion

Serve for a nutritious main course
with stuffed eggs: scoop out the
yolks from halved hard-boiled
eggs, mash with low-fat soft
cheese, French grainy mustard
and seasoning to taste, then pipe
or spoon back into the egg cavities.

Desserts and Baking

When you're thinking healthy and slim, you probably think that the sweet things in life are forbidden, especially biscuits and cakes. Fresh fruit, yogurt and low-fat cheese are the usual 'healthy' endings to a meal, but there's no reason why you should cut out sweet things altogether. The recipes in this chapter use wholefood ingredients — raw brown sugar, wholemeal flour, yogurt and fresh fruit — illustrating a point that you don't have to have wicked ingredients like chocolate, white sugar and cream to make delicious desserts.

GINGER FRUIT SALAD

| 0.30* | 86 cals |

* plus 1 hour macerating

Serves 4

2 apricots

2 dessert apples

1 orange

241 ml (8½ fl oz) bottle low-calorie ginger ale

50 g (2 oz) white grapes, seeded

2 bananas

30 ml (2 tbsp) lemon juice

1 Prepare the fruits to be macerated. Plunge the apricots into a bowl of boiling water for 30 seconds. Drain and peel off the skin with your fingers.

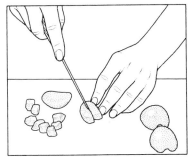

2 Halve the apricots, remove the stones and dice the flesh. Core and dice the apples, but do not peel them. Peel the orange and divide into segments, discarding all white pith.

3 Put the prepared fruits in a serving bowl with the ginger ale. Stir lightly, then cover and leave to macerate for 1 hour.

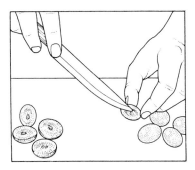

4 Cut the grapes in half, then remove the seeds by flicking them out with the point of a knife.

5 Peel and slice the bananas and mix them with the lemon juice to prevent discoloration.

6 Add the grapes and bananas to the macerated fruits. Serve in individual glasses.

Menu Suggestion
A refreshing end to any summer meal, Ginger Fruit Salad can also be topped with a spoonful of natural set yogurt.

GINGER FRUIT SALAD

If you wish to make this fruit salad in wintertime, then you can use dried apricots instead of the fresh ones suggested here. All the other fruits are available in winter.

Take a look at the wide choice of dried apricots at your local health food shop. The kind sold in packets in supermarkets are invariably bright orange in colour, which means that they are not necessarily naturally

dried apricots—their good colour may come from an edible dye, so check the ingredients on the label before buying. Dried apricots sold loose in health food shops are a much better buy, especially the *hunza* variety, which are sun-dried and can be eaten just as they are, without soaking. Sun-dried apricots are often sold with their stones still in; these should be removed before using in fruit salads.

STRAWBERRY CREAM

| 0.15* | 79 cals |

* plus 1 hour chilling

Serves 6

100 g (4 oz) cottage cheese
150 ml ($\frac{1}{4}$ pint) natural yogurt
clear honey, to taste
700 g (1$\frac{1}{2}$ lb) fresh strawberries

1 Work the cottage cheese in a blender or food processor until smooth. Alternatively, work through a fine wire sieve by pushing with the back of a metal spoon.

2 In a bowl, beat the cheese and yogurt together with honey to taste. Set aside.

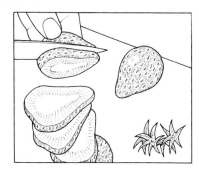

3 Hull the strawberries and slice finely, reserving 6 whole ones to decorate.

4 Divide the sliced strawberries equally between 6 individual glasses or glass serving dishes.

5 Pour the cheese mixture over the strawberries and chill in the refrigerator for about 1 hour. Serve chilled, decorated with the reserved whole strawberries.

Menu Suggestion
Strawberry Cream is rich and creamy in flavour yet surprisingly low in calories. Serve as a special summertime dessert, with langues de chat or wholemeal shortbread biscuits.

CRUNCHY PEARS IN CINNAMON AND HONEY WINE

| 1.00 | 230–344 cals |

Serves 4–6

60 ml (4 tbsp) white wine, vermouth or sherry

60 ml (4 tbsp) clear honey

5 ml (1 tsp) ground cinnamon

50 g (2 oz) margarine or butter

100 g (4 oz) wholewheat breadcrumbs (made from a day-old loaf)

50 g (2 oz) demerara sugar

4 ripe dessert pears

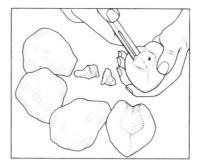

1 In a jug, mix together the wine, honey and half of the cinnamon. Set aside.

2 Melt the margarine in a small pan, add the breadcrumbs, sugar and remaining cinnamon and stir together until evenly mixed. Set aside.

3 Peel and halve the pears. Remove the cores. Arrange the pear halves, cut side down, in a greased ovenproof dish and pour over the white wine mixture.

4 Sprinkle the pears evenly with the breadcrumb mixture and bake in the oven at 190°C (375°F) mark 5 for 40 minutes. Serve hot.

Menu Suggestion
Accompany with yogurt flavoured with grated orange rind.

CRUNCHY PEARS IN CINNAMON AND HONEY WINE
For this recipe you can use Comice dessert pears, but be careful that they are not too ripe—Comice pears very quickly become over-ripe and bruised, and cannot be stored for any length of time. Buy them on the day you intend to cook them and check they are perfect and *just* only ripe before purchase. Conference pears are a dual-purpose pear; they are ideal for cooking and eating, so these too can be used for this recipe.

LEMON MUESLI CHEESECAKE

0.45* ✳* 317 cals

* plus at least 4 hours chilling;
freeze without decoration

Serves 6

175 g (6 oz) muesli

75 g (3 oz) margarine or butter,
   melted

3 lemons

1 sachet (scant 15 ml/1 tbsp)
   powdered gelatine

225 g (8 oz) low-fat soft cheese

150 ml ($\frac{1}{4}$ pint) natural yogurt

60 ml (4 tbsp) clear honey

2 egg whites

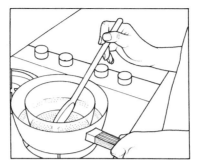

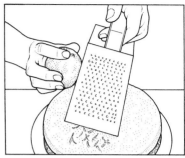

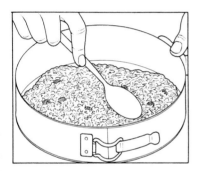

1 Mix the muesli and melted margarine together. With the back of a metal spoon, press the mixture over the base of a greased 20.5 cm (8 inch) springform cake tin. Chill in the refrigerator to set while making the filling.

2 Grate the rind of 2 of the lemons on the finest side of a conical or box grater. Set aside. Squeeze the juice from the 2 lemons and make up to 150 ml ($\frac{1}{4}$ pint) with water. Pour into a heatproof bowl.

3 Sprinkle the gelatine over the lemon juice and leave to stand for 5 minutes until spongy. Stand the bowl in a pan of hot water and heat gently, stirring occasionally, until dissolved. Remove the bowl from the water and set aside to cool slightly.

4 Whisk the cheese, yogurt and honey together in a separate bowl. Stir in the grated lemon rind and cooled gelatine until evenly incorporated.

5 Whisk the egg whites until standing in stiff peaks. Fold into the cheesecake mixture until evenly incorporated.

6 Spoon the mixture into the springform tin and level the surface. Chill in the refrigerator for at least 4 hours until set.

7 Coarsely grate the rind from the remaining lemon over the centre of the cheesecake, to decorate. Alternatively, slice the lemon thinly and arrange on top of the cheesecake. Serve chilled.

8 To serve. Remove the cheesecake from the tin and place on a serving plate.

Menu Suggestion
A luscious dessert for a special occasion, Lemon Muesli Cheesecake is made with healthier ingredients than other cheesecakes.

LEMON MUESLI CHEESECAKE

If you are buying muesli specially to make the base for this cheesecake, select a sugar-free variety, or at least one that is low in sugar. Health food shops sell muesli loose by the kg (lb), and most stock a sugar-free one. Recipes for muesli vary considerably from one brand to another—most health food shops mix their own, but the majority of muesli mixtures contain rolled oats, barley or wholewheat flakes and some dried fruit such as sultanas or raisins. You can of course make up your own muesli to suit yourself, or use the recipe on page 10. The addition of chopped hazelnuts gives extra nutritional value, and would be expecially good in the base of this cheesecake. As an alternative base, you could use crushed biscuits instead of muesli. Choose a wholefood-type, which are not too sweet—ginger biscuits would go well with the flavour of lemon. Put 175 g (6 oz) biscuits in a bowl and crush them with the end of a rolling pin. Use these crumbs exactly as for the muesli in the recipe.

BANANA WHIPS

| 0.20 | 208 cals |

Serves 4

2 egg whites

300 ml (½ pint) natural set yogurt

finely grated rind and juice of ½ orange

60 ml (4 tbsp) soft brown sugar

2 medium bananas

50 g (2 oz) crunchy breakfast cereal

1 Whisk the egg whites until standing in stiff peaks. Put the yogurt in a bowl and stir until smooth. Fold in the egg whites until evenly incorporated.

2 In a separate bowl, mix together the orange rind and juice and the sugar. Peel the bananas and slice thinly into the juice mixture. Fold gently to mix.

3 Put a layer of the yogurt mixture in the bottom of 4 individual glasses. Cover with a layer of cereal, then with a layer of the banana mixture. Repeat these 3 layers once more. Serve immediately.

Menu Suggestion
A quickly made dessert that appeals particularly to children of all ages.

RHUBARB BROWN BETTY

| 0.55 | ✳ | 228 cals |

450 g (1 lb) rhubarb

225 g (8 oz) fresh wholewheat
  breadcrumbs

50 g (2 oz) Barbados sugar

2.5 ml ($\frac{1}{2}$ tsp) ground ginger

50 ml (2 fl oz) fresh orange juice

300 ml ($\frac{1}{2}$ pint) natural yogurt,
  to serve

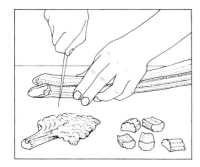

1 Trim the rhubarb and cut the
stalks into short lengths. Put in
a greased 900 ml (1$\frac{1}{2}$ pint) ovenproof dish.

2 Mix the breadcrumbs, sugar
and ground ginger together
and sprinkle over the fruit. Spoon
the orange juice over the crumbs.

3 Bake in the oven at 170°C
(325°F) mark 3 for 40 minutes
or until the fruit is soft and the
topping browned. Serve hot or
cold, with natural yogurt.

Menu Suggestion
Rhubarb Brown Betty is equally
good served hot or cold, with
natural yogurt. Any leftover will
also reheat well.

APRICOT OAT CRUNCHIES

0.45*	✳	166 cals

* plus overnight soaking and 1 hour cooling

Makes 12

75 g (3 oz) self-raising wholewheat flour

75 g (3 oz) rolled (porridge) oats

75 g (3 oz) demerara sugar

100 g (4 oz) margarine or butter

100 g (4 oz) dried apricots, soaked in cold water overnight

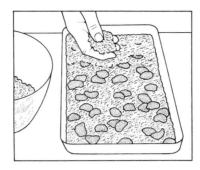

1 Lightly grease a shallow oblong tin measuring 28 × 18 × 3.5 cm (11 × 7 × 1½ inches).

2 Mix together the flour, oats and sugar in a bowl. Rub in the margarine until the mixture resembles breadcrumbs.

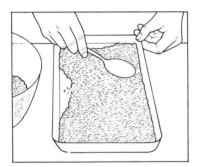

3 Spread half the mixture over the base of the prepared tin, pressing it down evenly.

4 Drain and chop the apricots. Spread them over the oat mixture in the tin.

5 Sprinkle over the remaining crumb mixture and press down well. Bake in the oven at 180°C (350°F) mark 4 for 25 minutes until golden brown. Leave in the tin for about 1 hour until cold. Cut into bars to serve.

Menu Suggestion
These delicious chewy teatime bars will keep well for several days if tightly wrapped in kitchen foil and kept in an airtight tin.

WHOLEWHEAT DATE AND BANANA BREAD WITH HAZELNUTS

2.00* ✳✳ **266–319 cals**

* plus cooling; freeze without honey and nut decoration

Serves 10–12

225 g (8 oz) stoned dates, roughly chopped

5 ml (1 tsp) bicarbonate of soda

300 ml (½ pint) milk

275 g (10 oz) self-raising wholewheat flour

100 g (4 oz) margarine or butter

75 g (3 oz) shelled hazelnuts, chopped

2 medium ripe bananas

1 egg, beaten

30 ml (2 tbsp) clear honey

1 Put the dates in a pan with the soda and milk. Bring slowly to boiling point, stirring, then remove from the heat and leave until cold.

2 Put the flour in a large bowl and rub in the margarine with your fingertips. Stir in the hazelnuts, reserving 30 ml (2 tbsp) for decorating.

3 Peel and mash the bananas, then add to the flour mixture with the dates and the egg. Beat well to mix.

4 Spoon the mixture into a greased and base-lined 1 kg (2 lb) loaf tin. Bake in the oven at 180°C (350°F) mark 4 for 1–1¼ hours until a skewer inserted in the centre comes out clean.

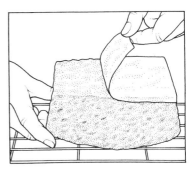

5 Leave the loaf to cool in the tin for about 5 minutes. Turn out, peel off the lining paper and place the right way up on a rack.

6 Heat the honey gently, then brush over the top of the loaf. Sprinkle the reserved hazelnuts on to the honey and leave until cold. Store in an airtight tin if not eating immediately.

Menu Suggestion
This lovely moist bread, more like a dense cake in texture, can be served unbuttered at tea time.

WHOLEWHEAT DATE AND BANANA BREAD WITH HAZELNUTS

It may seem unusual to have a cake made entirely without sugar, but this is because of the high proportion of dates used in this recipe. Dates have the highest natural sugar content of all dried fruit and if used in cakes such as this one there is no need to add extra sugar.

BRAN FLOWERPOTS

`1.45*` □ ✳ `813 cals*`

* plus 1½ hours rising and proving,
and 1 hour cooling; calories calculated
per loaf

Makes 3 loaves

25 g (1 oz) fresh yeast or 15 ml
    (1 tbsp) dried yeast and 2.5 ml
    (½ tsp) honey

600 ml (1 pint) tepid water

700 g (1½ lb) plain wholewheat flour

25 g (1 oz) soya flour

7.5 ml (1½ tsp) salt

40 g (1½ oz) bran

milk or water, to glaze

cracked wheat

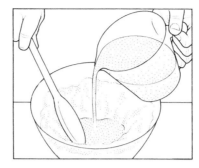

1 Choose 3 clean, new clay 10–
12.5 cm (4–5 inch) flowerpots.
Before using for the first time,
grease them well and bake in a hot
oven for about 30 minutes. This
stops the flowerpots cracking and
the loaves sticking. Leave to cool,
then grease again.

2 Blend the fresh yeast with the
water. If using dried yeast,
dissolve the honey in the water
and sprinkle over the yeast. Leave
the fresh or dried yeast liquid in a
warm place for about 15 minutes
until frothy.

3 Mix the flours and salt in a
bowl. Stir in the bran. Make a
well in the centre.

4 Pour in the yeast liquid and
mix to a soft dough that leaves
the bowl clean. Turn the dough on
to a lightly floured surface and
knead thoroughly for about 10
minutes until smooth and elastic.

5 Return the dough to the bowl,
cover with a clean cloth and
leave to rise in a warm place for
about 45 minutes or until the
dough is doubled in size.

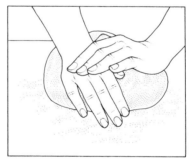

6 Turn the dough on to a
floured surface again and
knead for 10 minutes.

7 Divide and shape into the 3
greased flowerpots. Cover with
a clean cloth and leave to prove for
30–45 minutes until the dough has
risen to the top of the flowerpots.

8 Brush the tops lightly with
milk or water and sprinkle
with cracked wheat. Bake in the
oven at 230°C (450°F) mark 8 for
15 minutes, then reduce the oven
temperature to 200°C (400°F)
mark 6 and bake for a further
30–40 minutes until well risen and
firm. Turn out and leave to cool
on a wire rack for about 1 hour.

Menu Suggestion
Bran Flowerpots, with their
attractive shape will appeal
particularly to children. Spread
lightly buttered slices with a low-
sugar jam or a savoury spread such
as peanut butter (see page 141).

CAROB AND NUT CAKE

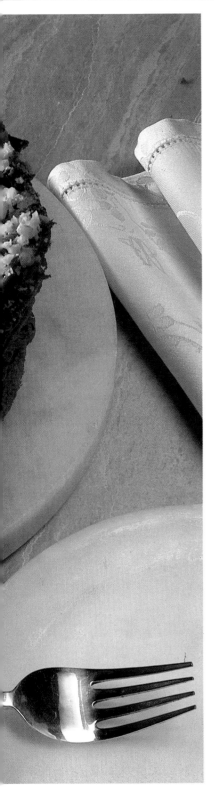

1.00*	✳✳	591–887 cals

* plus about 1¼ hours cooling; freeze
the cake plain, without filling or
topping

Serves 6–8

175 g (6 oz) margarine or butter

100 g (4 oz) soft brown sugar

4 eggs, separated

75 g (3 oz) plain wholewheat flour

25 g (1 oz) carob powder

pinch of salt

finely grated rind and juice of 1
    orange

two 75 g (2.65 oz) orange-flavoured
    or plain carob bars

75 g (3 oz) shelled walnuts, chopped

1 Put 125 g (4 oz) of the
margarine in a bowl with the
sugar and beat together until light
and fluffy. Beat in the egg yolks
one at a time.

2 Sift together the flour, carob
powder and salt, stirring in
any bran left in the sieve. Fold
into the creamed mixture with the
orange rind and 15 ml (1 tbsp) of
the orange juice.

3 Whisk the egg whites until
standing in stiff peaks, then
fold into the cake mixture until
evenly incorporated.

4 Divide the mixture equally
between 2 greased and base-
lined 18 cm (7 inch) sandwich tins.
Level the surface of the mixture,
then bake in the oven at 180°C
(350°F) mark 4 for 20 minutes or
until risen and firm to the touch.

5 Leave to cool in the tins for
1–2 minutes, then turn out
on to a wire rack and peel off the
lining papers. Turn the cakes the
right way up and leave to cool
completely.

6 Make the filling and topping.
Pour the remaining orange
juice into a heatproof bowl standing over a pan of simmering water.

7 Break the carob bars in small
pieces into the juice, then heat
gently until melted. Stir to
combine, then remove from the
heat and beat in the remaining
margarine. Leave to cool for about
10 minutes, stirring occasionally.

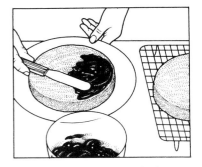

8 Spread half of the melted
carob mixture over 1 of the
cakes and sprinkle with half of the
walnuts. Top with the remaining
cake and swirl the remaining
melted carob over the top.
Sprinkle the remaining nuts
around the edge to decorate.

Menu Suggestion
Carob gives this tea time cake a
delicious chocolate flavour. Both
carob powder and carob bars are
obtainable from health food shops.

LEMON CAKE

| 1.15* | ⬦ | ✳ | 189 cals |

* plus 1 hour cooling

Serves 8

| 25 g (1 oz) margarine or butter |
| 30 ml (2 tbsp) milk |
| 3 eggs |
| 75 g (3 oz) Barbados sugar |
| 50 g (2 oz) plain wholewheat flour |
| 25 g (1 oz) bran |
| 5 ml (1 tsp) baking powder |
| finely grated rind of 1 lemon |
| 75 g (3 oz) plain quark (see page 140) |
| 10 ml (2 tsp) lemon juice |
| 25 g (1 oz) icing sugar |
| lemon slices, to decorate |

1 Grease and base-line two 18 cm (7 inch) sandwich tins. Grease the lining papers.

2 Put the margarine and milk in a small saucepan. Warm gently until the fat melts. Cool slightly.

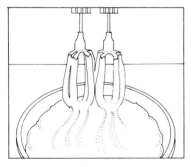

3 Put the eggs and sugar in a large bowl. Using an electric whisk, beat the mixture until very thick and light.

4 Fold in the flour, bran, baking powder and lemon rind. Gently stir in the cooled fat until evenly incorporated.

5 Divide the mixture between the prepared tins. Bake in the oven at 190°C (375°F) mark 5 for about 25 minutes until firm to the touch. Leave to cool for a few minutes in the tins then turn out on to a wire rack and leave to cool for about 1 hour.

6 Put the quark and lemon juice in a bowl. Sift in the icing sugar and beat together until evenly mixed. Use to sandwich the cakes together. Keep in a cool place until serving time. Decorate with the lemon slices.

Menu Suggestion
Ring the changes of the flavouring by substituting all or half the lemon rind and juice with orange.

USEFUL INFORMATION AND BASIC RECIPES

Eat Well, Eat Wisely

Some people already eat healthily but most of us could improve our diet by aiming to eat less fat, particularly saturated fat, sugar and salt and consume more dietary fibre. There is such a wide variety of natural ingredients to choose from for a healthy diet, that eating well and wisely will always be interesting and exciting.

INGREDIENTS FOR HEALTHY EATING

MEAT

In order to maintain a healthy, balanced diet, there is no need to become a complete vegetarian. There is, however, no need to eat meat every day. Three to four times a week should be enough, and then only at one meal during the day.

Meat is an excellent source of first class protein, which means that it does not have to be combined with any other ingredient in order to give you the right type of protein that your body needs.

Meat, and especially liver, is a rich source of B vitamins, in particular vitamin B12 which is essential for healthy red blood cells. Red meats and offal are rich in iron and the lighter meats in potassium.

Containing no carbohydrate or dietary fibre, all meats, even the leanest looking, do contain some fat. The fat in meats like lamb, pork and beef is mostly the saturated type, so try to eat less of these; choose lean cuts and eat more poultry and game which are relatively low in fat.

Try to eat liver or kidneys once every two weeks so that you benefit from their high iron content.

If possible, avoid all types of processed meats. These have a high salt, and very often high fat, content and most contain preservatives and other artificial ingredients.

Too many salty or smoked foods are not to be recommended, but a little ham or bacon occasionally will do no harm. Buy the leaner cuts and, for the best flavour and texture, cook the joints yourself.

Many people buy sausages for a quick and easy meal. To make sausages, meat is mixed in varying amounts with rusk, fat and soy protein. Before buying, check the meat content on the label, or ask your butcher exactly what his recipe for sausages contains. Avoid the pink coloured, smooth textured varieties. Look out, instead, for the natural coloured, herb-flecked types. Most sausages contain preservative. The butcher has, by law, to display a sign in his shop or to label them as such, if they do.

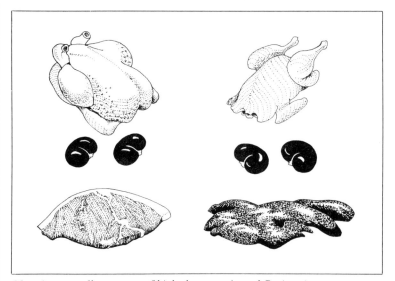

Meat is an excellent source of high class protein and B vitamins

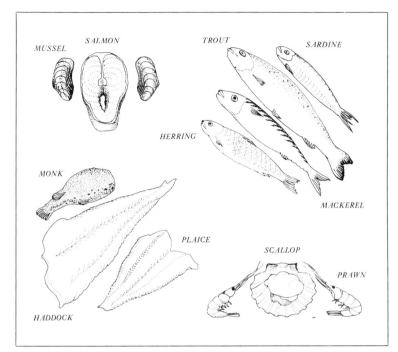

Fish and shellfish are protein-packed, and white fish are very low in fat

VEGETABLES

Fresh vegetables have a large part to play in a healthy diet. The different types provide a wide variety of vitamins and minerals, and all provide significant amounts of dietary fibre. If a selection are served at each meal, sometimes raw in a salad and sometimes cooked, you will obtain the best possible range of nutrients.

The vitamin most associated with vegetables is vitamin C, and this is found in the largest amounts in the green, leafy types.

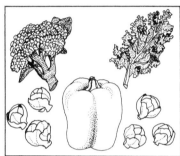

Green vegetables, rich in vitamin C

Broccoli, Brussels sprouts, kale and green peppers contain the most, closely followed by cabbage,

More vitamin C rich vegetables

cauliflower, mustard and cress and watercress. Potatoes are another good source and other types of vegetables contain smaller amounts.

Carotene, which is converted by the body into vitamin A, is to be found most often in vegetables

Most bought meat pies also contain a lot of fat. They are made with white flour and fillings may contain colouring and almost certainly preservatives and artificial flavourings. It is best to make them yourself using wholewheat flour.

Some butchers make their own pâtés from only natural ingredients. Other bought pâtés are not so nutritious. Read the labels and, if in doubt, make your own.

FISH

Fish and shellfish are a superb source of high quality, first-class protein and, like meat, need not be combined with other foods in order to supply the body with exactly the right type of protein that it needs.

There are basically two types of fish—white and oily. Both contain little or no carbohydrate and no fibre.

White fish are one of the few foods that contain iodine. They have an exceptionally low fat content since their natural oils are contained only in the liver.

The fat in oily fish is distributed throughout the flesh. It has a high proportion of poly-unsaturated fat and contains valuable amounts of vitamins A and D.

Most fish also contain small amounts of B vitamins, and varying amounts of the mineral zinc, which is found in only a few foods. Many shellfish are a good source of iron.

Fish products such as batter or bread-coated fish tend to be expensive; their coating is made from refined crumbs and often contains artificial colouring and in some cases preservative. It is better to coat and cook fresh fish fillets yourself, which is healthier and more economical.

Smoked fish should be eaten only occasionally. Not only does it have a high salt content, but some varieties such as mackerel and kippers are often artificially coloured brown or orange with a substance thought to be allergenic to some people.

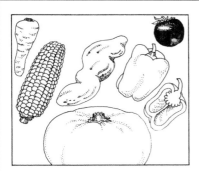

Vegetables high in carotene

that are red or orange coloured. Carrots in particular, are a good source, as are red peppers, pumpkin, tomatoes, sweetcorn and sweet potatoes. Green vegetables which also supply significant amounts include broccoli, curly

Green vegetables high in carotene

endive, kale, spinach, mustard and cress, watercress and avocados.

The B vitamins are also found in vegetables. Important amounts of vitamin B1 (thiamin) are contained in avocados, globe and Jerusalem artichokes, asparagus, broccoli, kale, mushrooms,

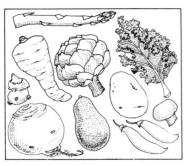

Vegetables rich in vitamin B1

parsnips, peas, potatoes and swedes.

Vitamin B2 (riboflavin) can be found in asparagus, runner and

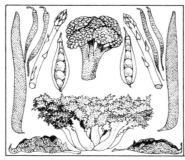

Vegetables rich in vitamin B2

French beans, broccoli, curly endive, peas and spinach.

There is no vitamin D in any vegetable, only tiny amounts if any, of vitamin E.

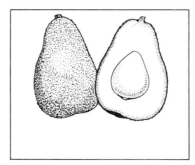

Avocados contain carotene

Vitamin K is found in varying amounts in all green vegetables.

The main mineral to be found in vegetables is calcium. There are

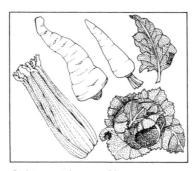

Calcium-rich vegetables

large amounts in cabbage and all leafy green vegetables, carrots, celery, spinach and parsnips. Iron is also to be found in green vegetables, in particular spinach and watercress. Mushrooms and peas are also good sources.

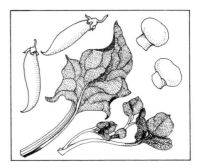

Vegetables high in iron

Most vegetables contain potassium, zinc and other minerals.

Carbohydrate is present in all vegetables, but the amounts vary widely. It is lowest in the leafy types and the seed-filled vegetables, such as cucumber and marrow. There are moderate amounts of carbohydrate in swede,

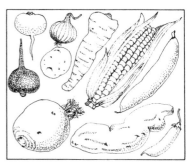

Vegetables containing carbohydrate

turnips and onions, and large amounts in potatoes, sweet potatoes, parsnips, beetroot, peas, broad beans and sweetcorn.

The only vegetable to contain more than a trace of fat is the avocado, and this fat is unsaturated. All vegetables, therefore, can be included in large amounts in a healthy diet.

Of the processed vegetables that

are available, frozen are more nutritious than canned. They have been quickly blanched and frozen, thus preserving as much of the vitamin content as possible.

Canned vegetables have often been cooked for a longer time and, in many cases, they are put into salted and sugared water. Their nutritional content can be lower than that of fresh vegetables. (However, if you feel that your store cupboard would be incomplete without a few cans of vegetables for emergency use, read the labels when buying.) Some are now packed without added salt and sugar.

PULSES

The term pulses covers all the various beans, peas and lentils which have been preserved by drying. Pulses have been used throughout the world for many centuries, but it is only recently that they have become an alternative protein food in the West.

In a vegetarian diet, pulses are an important source of protein, but to make the most of this they must be eaten with grain products. Proteins are made up of chains of substances known as amino acids. The amino acid chains in animal proteins (meat, fish, eggs, dairy products) are similar to those in our own bodies. When they are

eaten alone, they provide all the amino acids that we need. The proteins found in pulses are lacking in certain amino acids. These, however, are to be found in grain products. Therefore, a meal containing both beans and grains will provide protein that is just as good as a meat or fish meal.

Grain products to serve with pulses include wholewheat bread or pastry, brown rice, wholewheat

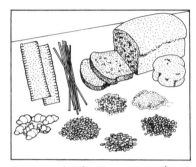

Grains and pulses to serve together

pasta, burghul wheat, buckwheat, oats and cornmeal.

Because of their need to be eaten with other ingredients in a meal, pulses are referred to as a 'second class' protein food, but this should not be considered in any way to their detriment.

The one exception to this rule is the soya bean, which contains the right type of protein in order to be served alone.

All pulses contain the B group vitamins, thiamin, riboflavin and niacin. Most contain significant

amounts of iron, potassium and calcium.

All but soya beans are fairly high in carbohydrates; and where the others contain only a trace of fat, soya beans contain 18–22% but this fat is mostly the unsaturated type.

There are many different types of pulses available at the moment and they can be bought from health food shops, ethnic shops and supermarkets. They include the large white butter beans, small white haricot beans and the pale green flageolets. There are four types of kidney bean: red, brown, black and the white kidney or cannellini beans. Black-eyed beans are small, kidney shaped and ivory with a black spot. Chick peas are round, with a slight point at one end and are usually cream coloured, although red and black varieties can be found.

The two smallest varieties are the maroon coloured aduki beans and green mung (or moong) beans.

Pinto beans are a speckly grey-pink colour and kidney shaped. Field beans, which are one of the most unusual, are round and the colour of horse chestnuts.

Soya beans are round and ivory or black coloured, becoming peanut shaped on soaking.

Split red lentils are still the most popular. There are also tiny brown Indian lentils, tiny grey ones, sometimes called puy, and slightly larger green or Egyptian lentils. All these types are sold

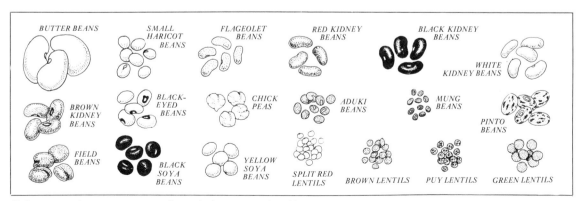

Pulses are an important source of protein in a vegetarian diet

whole and are eliptical in shape. Some Indian shops also sell white lentils.

All pulses should be stored in airtight containers, preferably in a cool, dark cupboard. They will keep for up to six months, after which, their skins toughen.

Apart from variations of timing, the cooking process for all beans is the same. First of all, they must be soaked, either overnight or by the quick-soak method.

It has recently been discovered that if certain types of beans are not properly cooked they can cause very severe stomach upsets. These include all types of kidney beans, pinto beans, flageolets, haricot and aduki beans. To render them harmless, they must at some time during their cooking process be boiled vigorously for at least 10 minutes. It is a good idea to build this into the soaking method when cooking any beans, so that it becomes an unforgettable habit.

To soak overnight, simply cover the beans with cold water. The next morning, drain them, bring to the boil in fresh water and boil for 10 minutes. Drain. Cook with fresh water.

For the quick-soak method, put the beans into a saucepan and cover with cold water. Bring to the boil and boil for 10 minutes. Cover the pan tightly and leave the beans in the same water for 2 hours. Drain and cook in fresh water for the specified time.

After soaking, simmer the beans in fresh water until they are tender. Mung and aduki beans need 45 minutes to 1 hour. Black-eyed beans need 1 hour. Kidney beans, haricot beans and flageolet need 2 hours and chick peas and soya beans up to 3 hours.

These times can be speeded up by using a pressure cooker.

Lentils and split peas need no soaking. (Red lentils and green and yellow split peas will cook to a purée in about 45 minutes. Whole lentils need 45 minutes to 1 hour to become soft.)

SOYA PRODUCTS

The versatile soya bean forms the base for many products which help to add protein to vegetarian and vegan (non-dairy) diets.

TAMARI SAUCE

This is a natural soy sauce made only from fermented soya beans and sea salt. (The cheaper kinds of soy sauce are made from soya bean extracts and contain caramel.) Tamari sauce can be used to flavour Chinese and Japanese dishes, salad dressings, barbecue sauces and many other vegetarian and non-vegetarian dishes. Buy it from health food shops and oriental grocers.

SHOYU SAUCE

This is another natural soy sauce. It is made from fermented soya beans, cracked wheat and sea salt. It, too, is available from health food shops.

MISO

This is a thick, dark brown paste, made from soya beans and grains such as whole barley or brown rice. It is high in protein and B vitamins with a flavour in many ways similar to beef extract.

Miso is used to enrich vegetable soups and stews, to which it must be added only for the last few minutes of cooking. The types of miso that you find are:
Hacho miso, made only from soya beans.
Mugi miso, made from soya beans and barley, and lighter in colour with a slightly less salty flavour.
Kome miso, made from soya beans and white rice, and salty.
Genmai, made from soya beans and brown rice, and slightly sweet.

TOFU

This is also known as soya bean curd and has always been an important ingredient in Chinese cooking. Recently it has become much more readily available in the West and is constantly being used in new and exciting dishes, both sweet and savoury.

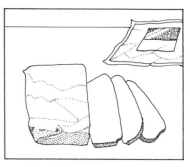

Tofu provides first class protein

Tofu looks rather like cheese in the early stages of making before the whey has been completely drained off. It is off-white in colour and is formed into soft blocks. Tofu can be bought by weight from Chinese stores or conveniently packaged into cartons from the health food shop.

Tofu provides a first class protein. It has relatively low carbohydrate and fat contents and is a good source of calcium, iron and the B vitamins, thiamin and riboflavin.

SOYA MILK

Soya milk is a substitute milk made from soya beans. It is sold in cartons and cans. Soya milk can be used and drunk in exactly the same ways as ordinary milk.

It contains protein, B vitamins, and some calcium, with no lactose or saturated fats. If possible, look out for the types of soya milk that do not contain added sugar.

SOYA FLOUR

This is made from ground, dried soya beans. It is a creamy yellow colour with a nutty flavour. It does not possess the rising properties of grain flours but up to 25% can be used in bread or pastry recipes to add extra protein without changing the original flavour. You must, if using soya flour, bake at a slightly lower tem-perature, since soya flour has a tendency to burn in a hot oven.

For those allergic to milk, soya flour and water can be made into a substitute white sauce.

THE BENEFITS OF VITAMINS

Vitamin A: For healthy skin and good eyesight.

Vitamin B group—main vitamins: Vitamin B1 (Thiamin), Vitamin B2 (Riboflavin), Niacin, Vitamin B12: Important for healthy blood and nervous system. They act as a catalyst, releasing energy from starch and sugar foods thus allowing full use of protein intake.

Vitamin C: As this vitamin is not stored by the body, we need to eat fruit and vegetables each day. Essential for healthy skin and body tissues.

Vitamin D: In most cases our requirement of this vitamin is manufactured in our bodies by the effect of sunlight on the skin. Calcium and phosphorus should be in the diet with Vitamin D. It is required for the growth and strength of bones and teeth, therefore particularly important for children, pregnant women and nursing mothers. Cod liver oil, halibut oil and vitamin preparations can be used in the correct dosage to supplement the diet.

Vitamin E: The need for this vitamin (in most foods) is not yet properly understood.

Vitamin K: This is made in the body and is present in many foods. Needed for blood clotting.

OTHER NUTRIENTS

Proteins Repair and renewal of tissue in adults; growth in children.

Fats Needed in small amounts for normal health. Vitamins A and D are fat soluble and are found in most foods with a fat content.

Carbohydrates Produce energy and heat. Small quantities needed for most people; more for those leading very active lives.

MINERALS

Calcium: Needed for healthy bones and teeth, as well as blood clotting and muscle functions. Vitamin D must be present for absorption of calcium.

Iron: Forms part of the red pigment of the blood which carries oxygen around the body. Also present in muscles. Important for women, since deficiency may cause anaemia.

TEXTURED VEGETABLE PROTEIN (TVP)

This is a highly processed product of the soya bean which is used as a meat extender or substitute. TVP is sold in dried form and re-constituted immediately when boiling water is poured over it.

Although it provides protein, TVP often contains artificial colourings and flavourings, and the cooked texture is not good. It is not necessary in a wholefood diet.

SOYA GRITS

Also called soya splits, these are made from cooked, cracked soya beans. In appearance, they look like small pieces of chopped soya bean. Soya grits need no soaking and will cook in 45 minutes, whilst providing the same nutrients as whole soya beans.

SAVA (vegan cheese)

This is an imitation hard cheese made from soya flour and a hard vegetable margarine. It is flavoured principally with yeast extract. Herb and/or garlic flavoured varieties are also available from some health food shops.

Sava is best eaten with fruit, bread or biscuits like ordinary cheese. It can also be used in cooking, although is not suitable for dishes such as pizzas as it does not have the good melting qualities of milk cheese.

FRUIT

The wide variety of fruits that are available all the year round provide a healthy and natural sweetness. Both fresh and dried fruits can be included in a wholefood eating programme every day, and at any meal.

FRESH FRUITS

Fresh fruits are an excellent source of dietary fibre and none contain more than a trace of fat.

Most fresh fruit contains significant amounts of vitamin C.

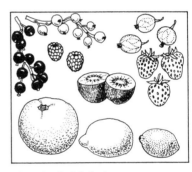
Vitamin C rich fruits

Blackcurrants contain the most and others with large amounts are strawberries, citrus fruit, red-currants, gooseberries, raspberries and kiwi fruit.

The amount of vitamin C is far greater when the fruit is eaten fresh. Cooking can destroy up to 50 per cent.

Carotene, which is converted to vitamin A in the body, is found in yellow-coloured fruit such as apricots (which have the highest count), mangoes, peaches and yellow melons. There is also a little vitamin A in blackcurrants, gooseberries and some other fruits.

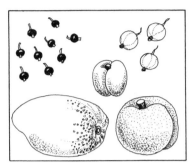

Vitamin A rich fruits

Small amounts of B vitamins can be found in fresh fruit. Citrus

Fruits containing thiamin

fruits, plums, pineapple, melon and bananas are the best sources of thiamin. Other B vitamins found in fruits include riboflavin, nicotinic acid, pyridoxine, pantothenic acid and folic acid.

No fruits contain vitamin D. Vitamin K is present in some fresh fruit, in particular the pith and white fibre of citrus fruit.

All fresh fruits contain carbohydrate in varying amounts. Those with a high carbohydrate count (over 10 g per 100 g) are fresh dates, bananas, grapes, apples, nectarines, cherries, greengages and pineapple. Those with 6–10 g per 100 g are cooking apples, damsons, fresh figs, plums, peaches, pears, medlars, mulberries, dessert gooseberries,

Fruits high in carbohydrate

oranges, tangerines, blackcurrants, passion fruit and kiwi fruit.

Those fruits with 5 g carbohydrate per 100 g or less include grapefruit, melons, cranberries, red and white currants, lemons, green gooseberries and loganberries.

Protein is found in only tiny amounts in most fruits. Those fresh fruits which contain slightly higher amounts than others

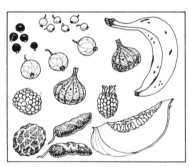

Fruits containing protein

include fresh dates, passion fruit, bananas, blackberries, red and white currants, figs, gooseberries, loganberries, melons and mulberries.

DRIED FRUITS

Dried fruits are full of concentrated goodness. Since most of the water content has been taken away, the amount of nutrients per 100 g (4 oz) is far greater than that of fresh fruits.

All dried fruits are an excellent source of dietary fibre and all contain only a trace of fat. Because of the drying process, none contain

more than a trace of vitamin C.

All dried fruits, except peaches and apricots, contain large amounts of thiamin (vitamin B1). Peaches and apricots, on the other hand, contain large amounts of carotene (which is converted to vitamin A). Prunes contain some but other dried fruit contain very little.

One of the values of dried fruits is their high mineral content. Potassium, calcium and phosphorus contents of most varieties are particularly high.

The carbohydrate content of all dried fruits is high. Unsoaked, it varies from 43–63 g per 100 g (about 2 oz per 4 oz).

All dried fruits contain small amounts of protein.

If possible, when buying dried fruits, choose the duller, stickier kinds that are usually sold in health food shops. The shiny fruits in sealed plastic packs, which are sold by supermarkets, are coated in a mineral oil, which is thought to be harmful. Should you buy this type of fruit, wash it well before using.

Do not buy more than one month's supply of dried fruit at a time. If stored for any longer, it may become dry looking and develop a sugary coating. This dried fruit can still be used successfully for cakes, but is not quite so effective for serving unsoaked or for making fruit compotes.

Store dried fruits in airtight containers in a cool, dark cupboard.

Dried fruits can be eaten raw as snacks and sweetmeats, and chopped into salads. They can also be reconstituted and used in desserts, mueslis and other dishes. Since boiling them destroys large amounts of the B vitamins (in particular thiamin), it is best to soak dried fruits in water or natural fruit juices for six hours or until they are soft. Use just enough liquid to cover them and either use the liquid in the final dish or save it for drinking.

DAIRY PRODUCE

MILK

Milk contains large amounts of calcium, plus other minerals including potassium, zinc and phosphorus. It is a good source of vitamin A, thiamin, riboflavin and other B vitamins. There is also some vitamin C. A useful amount of protein is present in milk and the amounts of fats and carbohydrate vary according to the type that you use. Ordinary unskimmed milk contains 11 g fat and 14 g carbohydrate per 275 ml ($\frac{1}{2}$ pint). The fats are 55% saturated fats and, therefore, if you have to follow a low-cholesterol diet, full cream milk should be used in moderation.

RAW MILK

This is whole milk that has not been subjected to any heat treatment. It is the most nutritious milk, since no vitamins have been destroyed by pasteurisation or heat treating. The fat and carbohydrate counts are the same as for ordinary whole milk. The availability of this milk depends on where you live.

WHOLE PASTEURISED MILK

The majority of the milk available is unskimmed and pasteurised. Pasteurising kills off bacteria; it involves the milk being heated to around 72°C (161°F), held for 15 seconds, rapidly cooled and then bottled. The process destroys some of the thiamin and a proportion of the vitamin C. The level of vitamin C in pasteurised milk further falls by 50% after 12 hours.

HIGH CREAM CONTENT MILK

This type of milk is produced from Channel Island and Devon cows. Its fat content is higher than that of ordinary milk, but it is also higher in vitamins A and D. The rich cream rises to the top and can be used as double cream. When mixed, this milk can make a lower fat substitute for cream in custards and mousses.

HOMOGENISED MILK

Homogenised milk is heat treated in a similar way to ordinary pasteurised milk. It is then further processed in order to break up the fat globules which then stay evenly distributed throughout the milk. Homogenised milk can therefore be frozen, but once thawed it should be used quickly and not refrozen.

STERILISED MILK

The heat treatment involved in producing sterilised milk takes it up to a temperature of around 100°C (212°F). It will remain fresh without refrigeration for up to a week, but half the vitamin C and one quarter of the thiamin are lost. The flavour is also affected. Sterilised milk is therefore not really the best of milks in a healthy diet.

ULTRA HEAT TREATED (UHT) MILK

This is homogenised milk which has been heated to a temperature of 135–150°C (275–300°F). Consequently, it will keep for up to six months. The heat treatment reduces the vitamin content and affects the flavour. UHT milk is a good standby to have for emergency use, but it is not the best quality milk to use regularly.

SKIMMED MILK

Probably the best to choose for a healthy diet, skimmed milk is pasteurised or UHT milk that has had virtually all its fat content removed, making the finished product lower in cholesterol and containing only half the calories of ordinary pasteurised milk. However, with the fats go the vitamins A and D.

SEMI-SKIMMED MILK

This is pasteurised or UHT milk with about half the fat content removed. It contains three quarters the calories and cholesterol of ordinary milk, but a smaller percentage of vitamins A and D.

SKIMMED MILK POWDER

This is produced from skimmed milk that has been spray dried. Once reconstituted with water, the product is nutritionally similar to liquid skimmed milk with a reduction in B vitamins.

FORTIFIED SKIMMED MILK POWDER

This is spray dried skimmed milk, enriched with vegetable fat and vitamins A and D. When reconstituted, it has a similar fat and vitamin content to ordinary pasteurised milk. The fat used is generally coconut oil which is a saturated fat.

EVAPORATED MILK

This has had its water content reduced from around 86% to 68%. Unless it has been skimmed before evaporation, it will have a higher fat and carbohydrate content than ordinary milk. The vitamin content will have been lowered and the flavour changed. Evaporated milk should not feature often in a healthy diet.

CONDENSED MILK

This is a considerably concentrated milk product with a high proportion of sugar. It should not be included in a healthy diet.

GOAT'S MILK

Goat's milk is becoming increasingly popular and easier to obtain. Compared to ordinary pasteurised milk, it has almost equal protein and carbohydrate counts but slightly more fat. The mineral content is higher, it has slightly more vitamin A and twice the vitamin D. The amount of vitamin C is about the same although, since the milk is not usually pasteurised, this does not diminish so rapidly.

The fat globules in goat's milk are smaller than in cow's and are evenly distributed throughout the milk, making it more easily digestible. This, and the fact that in constitution goats milk is nearer to human milk than cow's milk, makes it more suitable for babies of six months and onwards, and for anyone who may have a cows' milk allergy.

STORING MILK

Untreated and pasteurised milks should be kept in the refrigerator or a very cool larder. In the refrigerator they will keep for up to three days, in a larder for up to two.

Unopened sterilised milk will keep for up to one week unrefrigerated.

UHT milk will keep in a cool place for up to six months, but it is wise to check the date stamp. Once opened it should be treated like fresh milk.

Skimmed milk powder should be kept in a cool cupboard and used within three months once opened.

YOGURT

Yogurt is made by introducing two harmless bacteria, Lactobacillus bulgaricus and Streptococcus thermophilus, into either whole or skimmed milk. These bacteria feed on the milk sugars and produce an acid which coagulates the protein, resulting in the thick consistency of yogurt.

Vitamins and minerals remain similar in proportion to those in whole or semi-skimmed milk.

Yogurt is higher in protein than milk, but contains less vitamin A, unless this vitamin has been added artificially. It is richer in B vitamins and minerals and, since the milk sugars have been partially fermented, contains fewer carbohydrates.

Most natural or unflavoured yogurts on the market are 'live' to the extent that they all contain the two types of introduced bacteria and no pasteurisation or sterilisation has taken place. You will find sugar, which is used

mostly as a sweetener, on the ingredients lists of some brands.

Smaller brands of yogurt, that are more often to be found in health food shops, are also made from whole or skimmed milk. Different brands vary in texture and flavour because of the different methods of manufacture.

Some fruit yogurts have been pasteurised or sterilised after they are made. This prevents the fruit from fermenting but unfortunately it also removes 95% or more of the beneficial bacteria. Some smaller manufacturers sell live fruit yogurts. These obviously will have a shorter shelf life.

Many fruit yogurts also contain colouring and preservative, and most contain sugar.

If you wish to eat fruit yogurts it is best to make your own by mixing fruit purées into natural yogurts. To make your own yogurt see page 152.

USING YOGURT

Yogurt can be eaten at any time of the day and can be used in either sweet or savoury dishes.

It is particularly delicious served with breakfast cereal or muesli, and can make a refreshing summer drink as well as a convenient picnic food. As a dessert, serve it mixed with fruit purées, nuts, honey or sugar-free jam. Use instead of cream to top fruit salads and other desserts; or make light textured mousses, ice-creams and fruit fools.

Yogurt makes a perfect, low-fat salad dressing and is an excellent meat tenderiser when used in a marinade. Swirl it into soups, make into a sauce for grilled meats, use to top casseroles and stews or pour over white fish before baking.

When cooking with yogurt, care should be taken not to heat it too vigorously as it will curdle. Let the yogurt come to room temperature before adding to a hot dish and, if adding to a soup or sauce, whisk it into the hot liquid just before serving.

BUTTERMILK

Cultured buttermilk is made in a similar way to yogurt. It is more liquid than yogurt and is generally sold in 575 ml (1 pint) or 275 ml ($\frac{1}{2}$ pint) cartons. Buttermilk makes a refreshing drink, either straight from the carton or diluted with mineral water. Mixed into cakes and scones instead of milk, it makes them extremely light textured.

CHEESE

Most cheese is made by adding rennet or a similar substance and starter cultures to milk, which then separates into curds and whey. The whey is drained off and the further processing of the curds determines the final character of the cheese. The many different types of hard and soft cheeses available can all be included in a healthy eating pattern.

All cheeses are excellent sources of calcium. The other mineral present in significant amounts is phosphorus.

Vitamins A and D are present in all cheeses, but in greater amounts in the full fat types. Cheese is also an important source of the B vitamins, riboflavin, biotin and B12.

Most cheeses contain no carbohydrate at all. Cottage cheese contains a very small amount.

The fat content of cheese varies widely, depending on the manufacturing process and on whether full fat or skimmed milk has been used. Full fat hard cheeses, such as Cheddar, have a high fat content as do full fat soft and cream cheeses. There are medium fat cheeses such as Edam or curd cheeses, and low fat varieties including cottage cheese and quark.

The fat contained in cheese is 50–60% saturated and so consumption of the high fat types has to be watched carefully if you are following a low cholesterol diet.

The protein provided by cheese is a first class protein. This means that cheese does not have to be combined with any other ingredient in order to supply the body with every amino acid that it needs for healthy growth and repair. Weight for weight, cheese supplies more of this protein than meat or fish, so only small amounts, particularly of the hard types, are needed to make a nutritious meal.

Mature Cheddar will cost slightly more, but it has a stronger flavour and so only small amounts will make a dish that is both substantial and full of flavour. This will be better for your budget and better for your health.

When you buy hard cheese, it should look fresh with no dried areas or beads of fat on the surface. If it is pre-wrapped, it should not look moist or greasy or have any trace of mould.

If mature hard cheese is in good condition when it is bought and is securely wrapped in cling film or foil, it should keep for up to one month in a refrigerator. White Stilton should be eaten within a week. If you have no refrigerator, keep cheese in the coolest place possible, again wrapped in cling film or foil. It should keep for up to a week, depending on the outside temperature. Hard cheeses have a better flavour and texture if they are brought to room temperature before being eaten.

Hard cheese is one of the most useful and versatile ingredients in the kitchen. Use as a filling in wholewheat sandwiches or on top of wholewheat toast. Make cheese into salads, stir it into sauces, sprinkle over soups, casseroles and bean and pasta dishes, and make a meal of lightly cooked vegetables by scattering them with grated cheese and chopped nuts.

HARD CHEESES
Hard cheeses include all the hard English cheeses—Cheddar, Cheshire, Lancashire, Leicester, Double Gloucester, Wensleydale, Derby, Caerphilly and Stilton— plus others such as Gruyère, Parmesan, Pecorino, Emmenthal, Gouda, Edam and Jarlsberg.

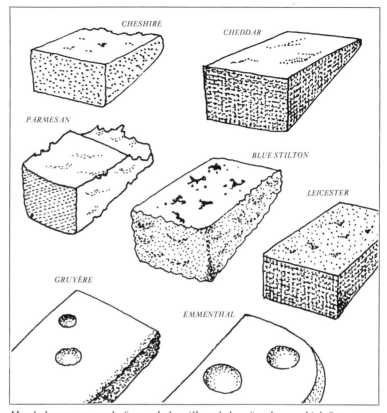

Hard cheeses are made from whole milk and therefore have a high fat content

Vegetarian cheeses are made with non-animal rennet. There are Cheddar and Cheshire types available in some health food shops and some supermarkets.

Most of the hard cheeses are made from whole milk and therefore have a high fat content.

Stilton has the highest fat count with 40 g fat per 100 g. Cheddar and Gruyère around 34 g and the

other hard cheeses around 30 g. Gouda has 26 g fat and Edam 22 g.

If you plan to cook with hard cheese and would rather buy the traditional product, it is best to buy the farmhouse or matured varieties. Hard cheese can also be added to breads, scones, pastries and pancakes and stirred into egg custards or fillings for quiches.

SOFT CHEESES
Soft cheeses include not only the creamy textured types that are sold in cartons, but the softer moulded cheeses such as Melbury or Camembert. Like the hard cheeses, their fat content varies widely.

Camembert, Brie, Melbury and Lymeswold have a fat count of around 23 g per 100 g.

Cream cheese contains a staggering 47 g fat per 100 g, and so should only be eaten occasionally.

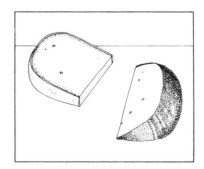

Gouda and Edam; medium fat cheeses

Curd cheese has a medium fat content. It has a smooth, creamy texture and is denser than most other varieties of soft cheese. Made from semi-skimmed milk, curd cheese has been produced by a natural souring process without the addition of rennet. It can be successfully substituted for cream cheese in many recipes. Thin curd cheese down with a little natural yogurt if you find it too stiff.

Cottage cheese is made from skimmed milk. It is therefore low in both fat and calories. Many varieties now contain preservative, so if you do not like your food to contain any artificial ingredients, it is best to always read the label.

Quark is a low or medium fat cheese, made by introducing a yogurt-type culture into the milk. Like curd cheese, it has a similar fat content, but has a fresher, lighter flavour.

To make your own quark, stir 30 ml (2 tbsp) natural yogurt into 1.15 litres (2 pints) ordinary pasteurised milk. Cover and leave in a warm place for 12 hours. Pour

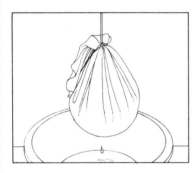

Making quark

the curds and whey into a scalded tea-cloth. Bring up the sides to make a bag. Hang it up to drip for 24 hours. Unwrap the cheese, turn it into a bowl and mix with a fork.

Fromage blanc is another continental cheese which has become very popular over the last few years. It is a low fat cheese with a rich, creamy flavour but a thin texture.

All soft cheeses should be stored in the refrigerator and

ideally eaten within three days of purchase.

Use them for dips, spreads and pâtés, beat them with eggs to make quiche fillings, use them to make

Spoon soft cheese over fruit

low fat mousses and sweet moulds; spoon them over fresh or stewed fruit.

VEGAN CHEESES
See under Nuts and Seeds (page 142) and Soya Products (page 135).

EGGS
Eggs are an excellent source of first class protein, containing a perfect balance of amino acids for growth and repair of body tissue. One egg will supply one tenth of the average adult daily protein needs.

Vitamins A and D are to be found in eggs, as are the B vitamins thiamin, riboflavin, biotin and B12 in significant amounts, and other B vitamins in smaller amounts. There is also a small amount of vitamin E.

The minerals contained in eggs include iron, calcium, potassium and magnesium.

Eggs contain only a trace of carbohydrate and 10.9 g fat per 100 g. Egg yolks are the single most concentrated source of cholesterol in our diet and most experts advise eating no more than 3–5 egg yolks (including those in made up dishes) a week. The fact that eggs are easy to eat and that so much goodness is packed into one small shell, they make an

excellent food for children, invalids and the elderly.

Most eggs are produced either in batteries or on the deep litter system, in which the hens are given free run of an enclosed shed. Only a small proportion are free-range and these tend to be more expensive.

Comparisons have been made between free-range and battery eggs. The levels of fat, protein and most of the B vitamins is more or less equal. Iron is higher in battery eggs as are calcium and sodium. Potassium is higher in free range. The amount of vitamin B12 is twice as high in eggs from free-range chickens and the folic acid (B6) content is 50% higher. This could be important for vegetarians since, apart from cheese, the only other major source of B12 is meat.

Store eggs, pointed end down, in a cool place or refrigerator and use them within one week of purchase.

NUTS AND SEEDS

Nuts and seeds, when mixed with whole grain ingredients, will provide a high protein meal.

They contain significant amounts of fibre whilst all but chestnuts have a low carbohydrate content.

All nuts and seeds are rich in minerals, particularly phosphorus, potassium, iron and calcium. In varying quantities, they also contain B vitamins and vitamin E.

With the exception of chestnuts, nuts and seeds have a high fat content. In some the fats are mainly polyunsaturated, in others they are monounsaturated (which seem to have little effect one way or the other on blood cholesterol) but in some, especially coconut, the fats are mainly saturated.

Most nuts and seeds are high in calories, but since only small amounts are usually mixed with grains to make vegetarian dishes, nut based meals need not be fattening.

All nuts and seeds should be sold when they are ripe and fully mature, and at the peak of their nutritional value. Shelled nuts may soon start to deteriorate after this, so never buy more than one month's supply at a time.

Store nuts in airtight containers in a cool, dark cupboard and chop or grind them as needed.

ALMONDS
Almonds are available in their skins, blanched, flaked and ground. If possible, always buy them with skins as once almonds have been processed they may lose

Skinning blanched almonds

some of their oils and natural flavours.

To blanch almonds, put them into a shallow pan and cover with cold water. Bring to the boil and remove immediately from the heat. Leave the almonds in the water, taking each one out separately and squeezing it out of its skin.

The fats contained in almonds are mostly monounsaturated. Their potassium, calcium, iron and magnesium content is high. They contain vitamin E and their carbohydrate count is low.

BRAZIL NUTS
Brazil nuts can be bought whole or in pieces. They contain large and almost equal proportions of saturated, polyunsaturated and monounsaturated fats.

The potassium, calcium,

magnesium and iron counts are high, and they contain small amounts of vitamin E.

CASHEW NUTS
Cashew nuts are low in most minerals apart from potassium. Their fat content is over 50% monounsaturated, the rest being made up of both saturated and polyunsaturated fats.

CHESTNUTS
Chestnuts can be bought fresh, dried or canned. To skin fresh chestnuts, slit the tops. Put them

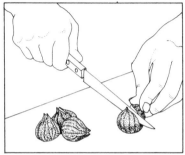

Preparing chestnuts to be skinned

into a saucepan of cold water and bring to the boil. Remove from the heat and leave the chestnuts in the water, taking each one out separately and peeling away the outer and inner skins.

To reconstitute dried chestnuts, soak them in cold water for 3 hours and then simmer in the soaking water for 30 minutes. Where a recipe calls for 450 g (1 lb) fresh, unpeeled chestnuts, use 225 g (8 oz) dried.

Canned chestnuts and unsweetened chestnut purée are useful storecupboard ingredients.

Unlike most other nuts, chestnuts are low in fats but high in carbohydrates. They are also lower in calories than other nuts. They are high in potassium and contain small amounts of B vitamins.

COCONUT
The fats in coconuts are almost all saturated fats. The protein content

is high. So, too, is the amount of potassium and iron. There are small amounts of calcium, magnesium and only traces of some B vitamins.

To check that a coconut is fresh when bought, shake it to make sure it contains plenty of liquid.

Desiccated and shredded coconut and coconut chips can be bought in most health shops. These have a higher food and calorie value by weight than fresh coconut.

Toasted coconut chips contain added Barbados sugar.

HAZELNUTS
Hazelnuts are rich in both calcium and vitamin E, and the B vitamins, folic acid and pantothenic acid.

Approximately 75% of the oil content is monounsaturated.

Toasted chopped hazelnuts can be bought in health shops and some supermarkets. These are useful for sprinkling over cakes and desserts as they have a slightly sweet flavour.

PEANUTS
Peanuts are technically not nuts at all but members of the pulse family. As they can be eaten raw, they are classed with nuts.

Peanuts are high in protein, but like the other pulses, must be served with a whole grain product.

Their fat content is 49 g/100 g and made up of about 50% monounsaturated, 35% polyunsaturated and the rest saturated.

They are high in potassium and iron, contain small amounts of most of the B vitamins (with the exception of B12) and some vitamin E.

PEANUT BUTTER
This is made from ground peanuts. Spread on wholewheat bread, it can provide a first class protein meal. If possible, buy the types that contain no salt or preservatives (usually available from health food shops).

PECAN NUTS

These are similar in shape to walnuts, only more elongated. The shells are a smooth, shiny red.

Pecans are high in potassium, calcium, magnesium and iron, and also contain significant amounts of zinc. They contain traces of B vitamins and carotene and a small amount of vitamin C. The larger proportion of their oil is mono-unsaturated and the rest mostly polyunsaturated.

PINE NUTS

Pine nuts are high in protein, calcium, iron and the B vitamin niacin. The larger proportion of their fats is monounsaturated, while most of the remainder is polyunsaturated.

PISTACHIO NUTS

Pistachio nuts are exceptionally high in protein, iron and potassium, and contain small amounts of most B vitamins. The larger proportion of their fats is monounsaturated.

WALNUTS

Walnuts are high in potassium, calcium, magnesium, iron and zinc. They contain small amounts of B vitamins, a trace of vitamin E, and are high in protein. Walnut oil is the highest in polyunsaturates of all nuts.

PUMPKIN SEEDS

White, grey and green varieties of pumpkin seeds are available. They are exceptionally rich in iron and calcium, and their protein content is high. They contain large amounts of the B vitamin niacin and small amounts of other B vitamins. Their fats are mostly polyunsaturated.

SESAME SEEDS

These are tiny, flat, tear-drop shaped seeds and vary from a pale cream colour to black. They are often sprinkled over breads and salads. Sesame seeds can be used as they are or toasted until golden

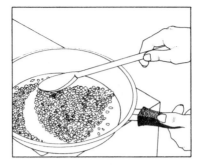

Toasting sesame seeds

in a dry frying pan over a medium heat.

These seeds are exceptionally high in protein, potassium, calcium and the B vitamin niacin, and contain significant amounts of the other B vitamins. The larger proportion of their fats are poly-unsaturated and they are rich in lecithin.

TAHINI

This is a paste made from ground sesame seeds. There are pale grey and dark grey varieties, the paler one having the finer flavour.

Use tahini for salad dressings, sauces and sandwich fillings, and for making bean pâtés and dips such as humus.

SUNFLOWER SEEDS

Sunflower seeds are small, pale grey coloured, tear-drop shaped seeds with a creamy flavour.

They are exceptionally high in protein, calcium, magnesium, iron and potassium. These seeds contain significant amounts of most B vitamins and a large amount of vitamin E. The larger proportion of their fats is polyunsaturated.

NUT CHEESE

An imitation hard cheese can be made from ground nuts and hard vegetable margarine with a little yeast extract for seasoning.

It can be eaten with fruit, bread or biscuits and in cold dishes and salads. It is not suitable for cooking as it does not have the melting qualities of dairy cheese.

GRAINS AND GRAIN PRODUCTS

All grains contain protein and, when mixed with other second class protein ingredients such as nuts or pulses, will provide good quality protein for healthy growth and repair of body tissue.

The B vitamins and minerals such as calcium, iron and copper are to be found in all grains and some contain vitamin E.

One important constituent of grains and grain products is dietary fibre. This is only present in useful amounts when the grains are unrefined, that is, when their outer coating, or bran, is left intact.

WHEAT

Wheat is one of the most used grain in the Western world. The whole wheat grain is made up of

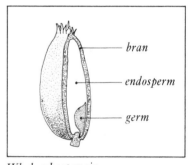

Whole wheat grain

the bran, the endosperm, or starchy part, and the germ, which is the most nutritious but which makes up only 2% of the grain.

Contained in the germ are most of the vitamins of the B group, a large amount of vitamin E, and minerals such as calcium, potassium, iron, copper and magnesium.

Wholewheat grains These can be cooked to make an accompani-ment to a main meal or a sweet dish such as the old English frumenty.

Sprouting wheat grains will lessen the carbohydrate content but will provide vitamin C.

Wheat bran This is the outer coating of the wheat grain. Adding extra bran to bread mixtures, sprinkling it over cereals and into drinks will greatly increase your fibre intake. However, it is far healthier if you can obtain all your fibre from wholemeal bread and other wholegrain products and from fruits, vegetables and pulses.

Wheat germ Wheat germ is the tiny nutritious part that has been separated from the main grain. It is consequently a highly concentrated source of B vitamins, vitamin E and minerals. If untreated, store in the refrigerator to prevent rancidity. Treated or stabilised wheat germ has been processed to prevent this.

Wheat germ can be sprinkled over sweet dishes and cereals, and used in crumble toppings, coatings and gratin dishes. It can also be added to pastry, cake and bread mixes.

Wheat flour Wheat flour is produced by grinding the wheat grain. Wholemeal (also called wholewheat) flour contains the whole (100%) of the wheat grain, with nothing added and nothing taken away. It therefore contains all the nutritious substances of the wheat germ and all the bran.

Brown flour (also called wheatmeal) flour has had a proportion of the bran removed, therefore making it lower in fibre but more suitable for lighter baked goods such as flaky pastry. Most of the wheat germ is still present.

White flour is a 70% extraction of the wheat grain. It consists mostly of the endosperm or starch and contains very little bran. Certain B vitamins and calcium have by law to be added back, but they are not in the original proportions. Most white flour has also been chemically bleached to make it a pure white colour.

Unbleached white flour is a

THE FIBRE FACTOR

Dietary fibre (roughage) is found only in plant foods. It is indigestible and remains in our intestine after other nutrients have been absorbed. While it seems odd that something of no nutritional value should be so important, fibre plays a vital role in keeping our bodies healthy. It prevents constipation and may also prevent certain disorders like cancer of the colon and diverticulosis. Fibre works by holding a lot of water so eating enough results in soft, bulky waste matter which is easy for the intestine to push along without pressure or straining. Potentially harmful substances are also diluted and eliminated quickly from the body so spend less time in contact with the wall of the intestine. The fibre in cereals is particularly good at holding moisture but that in other vegetable foods has its own protective effect and it is sensible to eat fibre from a variety of different sources. There is no recommended daily intake for dietary fibre but most experts agree that a healthy diet should contain at least 30 g (1 oz) a day.

However, there's no need to add bran to everything, simply eat more foods that are naturally high in fibre like wholegrain cereals (including wholemeal and some brown breads), breakfast cereals like Shredded Wheat, Weetabix and some mueslis), wholewheat pasta, brown rice, fresh fruit and vegetables and pulses.

70% extraction flour that has not been chemically bleached.

Strong flour is flour produced from hard wheat, giving it superior bread making qualities. Some wholewheat flours contain a proportion of hard wheat, making them suitable for both bread and other baking purposes.

Granary bread meal contains malted grains of wheat and rye. The flour base is usually of 85% extraction and contains added gluten to make a lighter loaf.

Stone ground flour has been ground slowly between old fashioned mill stones. Slow grinding produces less heat and therefore destroys fewer vitamins. Most other flours are ground very fast on a roller mill. It is also possible to buy flour which has been slowly ground on rollers in order to maintain goodness.

Wheat breads Wholemeal (wholewheat) bread is made only from wholewheat flour. Brands sold by large commercial companies may contain preservatives and stabilisers.

Brown or wheatmeal breads contain anything from a 75% to

an 85% extraction flour. Some may contain caramel in order to increase the brown colour.

Wheat germ breads are usually made from an 81% or 85% extraction flour with added wheat germ.

Granary breads are made from granary bread meal.

Cracked or kibbled wheat This consists of whole wheat grains broken or ground into coarse pieces. It is most often used as a decorative topping for wholewheat breads. This wheat can be cooked and served as an accompaniment to the main meal or it can be added to bread mixes to make a loaf with a grainy texture.

Burghul wheat Also called bulgur or bulgar wheat, this is made from whole wheat grains that have been soaked and then baked until they crack into small yellow particles.

To use, soak the wheat in warm water for 20 minutes. Drain and squeeze dry. Mix the wheat with an oil and vinegar dressing and add other ingredients such as parsley, olives and tomatoes to make a salad.

Preparing burghul wheat

Burghul wheat can also be cooked. Allow 600 ml (1 pint) liquid to 225 g (8 oz) wheat and cook until it has all been absorbed.

Wholewheat pasta All pasta is made from a special hard, high protein wheat called durum wheat, grown mostly in North America. Wholewheat pasta is made from the whole part of the wheat grains. Many different types are now available. Cook wholewheat pasta in the same ways and for the same amount of time as white pasta.

Wholewheat semolina Semolina is a coarsely ground flour produced from durum wheat. The wholewheat variety makes tasty milk puddings. It can also be soaked and served as a salad in the same way as burghul wheat. After adding the salad dressing, leave for 30 minutes.

Storing wheat products Wholewheat grains will keep for up to a year but once ground should not be kept for longer than one month if the full vitamin E value is to be maintained.

The exceptions are pasta and burghul wheat which will keep for up to 3 months.

Store all wheat products in a cool dark place in airtight containers.

OATS

Oats are high in protein, potassium, calcium, magnesium, iron and zinc, and contain small amounts of most B vitamins.

Oat groats These are whole oat grains. They can be cooked in a similar way to rice.

Oatmeal Whole oat grains are ground to make a meal of varying textures.

Pinhead oatmeal is the coarsest. Soaked overnight and cooked gently in the morning, they make a superb porridge.

Medium oatmeal and fine oatmeal are used for baking. Used alone, they make crisp oatcakes and bannocks. They can also replace up to one quarter of the flour when making bread or scones.

Rolled oats These are used mainly for muesli. They are produced by steaming and rolling either whole or pin-head oats. Use them also in flapjacks and crumble toppings.

Porridge oats These have been rolled and then partially cooked before being cooled and dried.

Instant oats These are made from a mixture of oatflakes and refined oat flour. They are not as nutritious and do not contain the same proportion of bran as do the other types.

Storing oat products Whole oat grains should keep for up to a year. Oat products quickly become rancid and should not be kept for longer than one month. Store them in a cool, dark place in airtight containers.

BARLEY

Barley contains large amounts of calcium, potassium and magnesium, and a certain amount of iron. It is high in the B vitamin niacin and contains small amounts of other B vitamins.

Pot barley This is the barley grain with only the rough outer husk removed. It is also called Scotch or hulled barley. Pot barley can be bought in some health food shops. Cook in the same way as brown rice and use to enrich casseroles.

Pearl barley This has both outer layers removed and so does not have the fibre content of pot barley.

Barley flakes These are made in the same way as rolled oats and are sold separately besides being included in some muesli mixtures.

Barley flour Unrefined barley flour can be bought from some health shops. Use it to make light pastries or to replace up to half the flour in bread and cakes.

RYE

Rye is rich in potassium, calcium, magnesium, iron and zinc, and contains small amounts of B vitamins.

Rye groats These or whole rye grains are found in some health food shops. They can be cooked as a single grain but need a long cooking time.

Rye flour Dark and light rye flours are available, the dark containing more bran. Rye flour has a delicious nutty flavour but contains only a small proportion of gluten. It should therefore be mixed half and half with wholewheat flour when making bread.

RICE

Whole grain rice, known as brown rice, has its outer coating of bran intact. Both long and short grain types are available.

Brown rice is rich in fibre and contains more iron, calcium, protein, niacin and thiamin than the white varieties.

The cooking time is longer than for white rice, usually 40–45 minutes. The methods of cooking are the same, although brown rice cannot be cooked in a steamer in the Chinese manner.

Rice flakes These make superb milk puddings. Brown rice flakes are available from some health food shops. The white variety contains few nutrients.

Rice flour 100% whole brown rice flour is available from some health food shops.

Rice bran Again available from health food shops, this is the outer layer of the grain removed in the production of white rice. It is an excellent source of B vitamins and fibre and can be used as wheat bran.

BUCKWHEAT

Buckwheat consists of tiny, brown heart-shaped seeds. They are high in protein, phosphorus and potassium, and contain most of the B vitamins. The grains are gluten free and so useful in a gluten restricted diet.

Buckwheat is usually lightly toasted and cooked to make the dish called kasha which has a pungent, nutty flavour.
Buckwheat flour This is a fine and grey coloured flour. It is used for making pancakes. In a gluten-free diet, buckwheat flour can be used for bread and cakes although these will not rise in the same way as those made with wheat flour.
Buckwheat spaghetti This is made from a mixture of buckwheat and wholewheat flours giving a pleasing nutty flavour. Buckwheat spaghetti cooks more quickly than wholewheat or white spaghetti.

MILLET

Millet takes the form of tiny, round, pale yellow seeds. It is rich in protein, calcium, iron and the B vitamins thiamin, riboflavin and nicotinic acid. It is very quickly cooked and can be served as an accompaniment or stuffing. Millet can also be mixed with nuts and pulses to make a main protein meal.

MAIZE
(corn or Indian corn)

Maize consists mainly of carbohydrate and contains more carotene than any other grain. It also contains significant amounts of potassium, calcium and iron, niacin and traces of other B vitamins.
Popcorn Dried maize which expands and softens when heated.

Maize meal or cornmeal Coarse yellow flour made from a 95% extraction of the maize and therefore high in nutrients and fibre. Use it to make corn bread, the Italian 'porridge' called polenta or for Mexican tortillas.
Cornflour (cornstarch) This is made from the starch of the corn kernels. It is a useful thickening agent but contains virtually no fibre or important nutrients.

TRITICALE

This is a cross between wheat and rye. The whole grains are sold mainly for sprouting.

Triticale flour is available in America.

FATS AND OILS

For a healthy diet, it is best to east less of all fats and oils. In particular, eat less butter, block margarine, lard, suet and other shortenings. Switch to soft margarines with a low saturated fat content, and pure vegetable oils, but try to cut down on these too.
Butter Butter is an animal product and therefore contains a high proportion of saturated fats. However, it is made simply by churning cream and then usually adding a little salt. There are no artificial additives or chemical processes involved.

Butter also contains vitamins A and D, calcium and small amounts of iron and magnesium. There is only a trace of carbohydrate.
Margarine All margarines are 80% fat and contain about the same calories as butter.

Margarines are made from animal, fish or vegetable oils either combined or singly.

If 'edible oils' appears on an ingredients list, the margarine probably contains a mixture of animal and vegetable fats.

Generally the harder the margarine, the greater the proportion of saturated fats it

contains. These need not necessarily be animal fats but vegetable fats that have been artificially saturated. Margarines with a high proportion of polyunsaturated fats are very soft.

Most margarines also contain whey solids, a little salt, water, lecithin, emulsifiers which help the oils mix with the water (these may be chemical or of natural origin), colouring, flavouring and vitamins A and D which must be added by law.

The best margarine for health is a soft margarine (low in saturated fat) made solely from vegetable oils.
Low-fat spreads These are made with similar ingredients to those of margarine, with extra water added. They are lower in fats and calories than ordinary margarine or butter.
Lard Lard, including the soft types, has a high proportion of saturated fats and should be used in moderation, if at all.
Shortenings or white fats These are a mixture of different types of fats that have been chemically re-fined and whipped. They are highly saturated, contain little goodness and should not be included in a healthy diet.
Creamed coconut Creamed coconut is pure coconut oil which is sold in the form of a white block. It can be used for frying, for enriching vegetable curries and as a cream substitute in sweet dishes.

Although creamed coconut is a pure vegetable product, it has a high proportion of saturated fats and should only be used in moderation.
Vegetable oils Most vegetable oils are high in polyunsaturated fats and low in saturated fat, making them ideal for cooking and for salad dressings. Safflower and sunflower oils contain the most polyunsaturated fats. Olive oil contains mostly monounsaturated fats and coconut oil is the only one high in saturated fats.
Other oils to buy are corn, soya

and groundnut. Walnut and sesame oils are excellent but more expensive.

Oils labelled simply 'vegetable' or 'cooking' oil contain a mixture of oil, including rape seed oil, can be quite high in saturated fat, and have a poor flavour.

Cold pressed oils are produced by pressing the nuts or seeds to extract their oils. They are deep amber coloured with strong, nutty flavours.

Store in a cool dark place and once opened, all oils should be used within one month.

SUGARS AND SWEETENERS

Manufactured sugar is the one ingredient that is totally unnecessary in a healthy diet. It is high in calories and although these calories are no more fattening than those from other foods, sugar has very little bulk so it is easy to eat a lot. Sugar also contains no other nutrients (some brown sugars contain tiny amounts of certain vitamins and minerals but the quantities are insignificant) and it is far better to get energy from foods that supply a range of nutrients and are bulky enough to satisfy hunger. Sugar is also bad for teeth, particularly when eaten in sticky forms like cakes, biscuits and sweets; the more frequently sugar is eaten the more harm it does.

White sugar White sugar is virtually 100% sucrose, contains no minerals and should be avoided whenever possible.

BROWN SUGARS

Demerara sugar True demerara sugar is produced from sugar cane. Its large, golden, slightly sticky crystals contain traces of vitamins and minerals. True demerara sugar should have its country of origin on the packet but no ingredients list.

London demerara sugar This is white sugar that has been coloured brown with a thin coating of molasses. This will be stated on the packet by way of an ingredients list.

Barbados sugar Barbados or Muscovado sugars are also referred to as raw sugars. The granules are small and the overall sugar soft and sticky. Both light and dark varieties are available. Barbados sugar is produced from the sugar cane which has been less refined than in the production of white or demerara sugars. Both light and dark varieties contain traces of B vitamins and minerals.

Soft brown sugar This is often bought in mistake for the Barbados sugars. It is in fact made from fine grain white sugar and sugar syrups, and contains no useful nutrients. There should be a list of ingredients on the pack.

Molasses sugar Also called black Barbados or demerara molasses. This is the least refined of all the sugars. It is very dark and sticky, and contains small amounts of B vitamins and minerals. It has a strong molasses flavour and is best used in baking.

SUGAR SUBSTITUTES

Molasses Molasses contains all the goodness of the sugar cane that is discarded in the production of white sugar. It includes minerals, B vitamins and about two thirds the calories of white sugar. It is a thick, black syrup with a strong flavour and so a little goes a long way.

Black treacle This is a more refined product than molasses although it has a very similar flavour and texture. It contains some minerals and B vitamins but not as many as molasses.

Golden syrup This is white sugar that has been melted and treated so that it does not re-crystallise. It has no significant nutritional value.

Honey Honey has been credited with many properties, but even so it does contain about 80% sugars and so should be eaten in moderation. Its flavour is richer and sweeter than that of sugar so you do not need to use so much.

Honey consists of 80% sugars, (mainly in the form of fructose and glucose), 20% water and the small amounts of some vitamins.

Honey also contains just over two-thirds the calories of sugar.

Maple syrup This is produced by tapping the sap of North American maple trees and considerably reducing it. It therefore contains a high proportion of sugar, but is also a rich source of minerals such as calcium, phosphorus, potassium and sodium.

Maple syrup is a fairly thin, dark red-brown syrup and, once opened, is best kept in the refrigerator.

Malt extract This thick, sticky, brown syrup produced from germinated barley grains consists mainly of maltose. It also contains small amounts of protein, B vitamins and minerals.

Pear and apple spread This is a thick, partially set, dark brown syrup produced by highly concentrating the juices from apples and pears. It contains fewer calories than sugar and more nutrients. Use this syrup as a spread, as a sweetener for some drinks and in baking.

Concentrated apple juice This is a thick, dark brown liquid again produced by concentrating natural apple juice. It can be used for drinks and to sweeten desserts and some baked goods.

Sugar-free jam This is made from fruits, fruit juices and natural pectin, and comes in a variety of different fruit mixtures. It can be used in the same way as ordinary jam since it is just as sweet but most are much lower in calories.

Fructose Fructose resembles fine icing sugar. It is far sweeter than normal sugars, so less can be used, thus reducing the calorie levels of anything made from it. Fructose contains little goodness and should not be necessary in a healthy diet.

Artificial sweeteners Artificial sweeteners are man made. Weight for weight, most are many times sweeter than sugar with no or few calories. Artificial sweeteners include saccharine, aspartame and acesulfame K.

Sorbitol, the artificial sweetener produced for diabetics, is made from glucose and so supplies calories. Eating too much (more than about 60 g (2 oz) a day) may have a laxative effect.

SALT AND SALT SUBSTITUTES

A small amount of salt (sodium chloride) is essential for maintaining bodily health. However, too much salt (or rather the sodium part of salt) is thought to lead to high blood pressure in certain individuals with an inherited tendency to develop this disorder. So it is advisable to eat less salt by using less in cooking and at the table as well as eating fewer salty foods.

Rock salt This is salt taken from underground deposits. It has fairly large granules which, when roughly crushed and sold for use in salt mills and for cooking, tend to compress together.

Table salt Most table salts are produced from rock salts that have been finely ground and mixed with a small proportion of magnesium carbonate to make them run freely.

Iodised salt This has iodine salts added and is recommended in areas with a natural iodine deficiency.

Sea salt This is produced by the evaporation of sea water. It may be fine or coarse crystals or in flakes. Some fine varieties have magnesium carbonate added.

Salt substitutes These are mostly produced from potassium salts and are useful in some cases of high blood pressure but check with your doctor first.

Sesame salt (gomasio) This is a useful substitute for ordinary salt. It is made by grinding together five parts roasted sesame seeds to one of either pure rock salt or sea salt.

CHOCOLATE AND CAROB

Cocoa powder Cocoa powder is made from the cocoa bean. It is rich in iron but contains caffeine and has a bitter flavour which needs to be tempered by a sweetener. It is quite high in fat, carbohydrates and calories.

Chocolate Chocolate is basically made from cocoa beans, milk and sugar. It must contain at least 35% dry cocoa solids and a minimum of 18% cocoa butter. Chocolate is high in fats and sugar, and contains traces of carotene and of some B vitamins and minerals.

Carob powder This is produced from the carob bean (also known as the locust bean) and is naturally sweet. It contains vitamins A and D, some B vitamins and minerals such as calcium and magnesium. It also includes protein and a small amount of fibre. Carob powder contains less fat and sodium than cocoa, fewer calories and no caffeine. Because of its sweet flavour, you need less sugar or other sweetener in order to make it taste pleasant.

Carob bars These are made in a similar way to chocolate bars. Most contain sugar but sugar-free brands are available.

CONVENIENCE FOODS

Using the occasional packet of frozen vegetables or fruit or can of sweetcorn will do no harm if, for most of the time, your diet is based on fresh products. Other products which may help out in emergencies are the cans of fruit in natural juices without sugar, but it is best not to use them regularly.

Manufactured goods such as pies, instant desserts and even batter-coated fish all contain preservatives, and in many cases artificial flavourings. Their fat, sugar and salt content is also often high. Manufactured goods of this type should feature only occasionally in a healthy diet.

Healthy Cooking

Buying only fresh and natural foods is only the beginning. In the kitchen, you can help yourself to eat healthily by employing lighter cooking methods which involve only a little fat and no rich sauces.

COOKING METHODS

GRILLING

Grilling is a cooking method which is suitable for meat and fish, and also some vegetables.

MEAT

As it is a fairly quick way of cooking, you need only the best quality meats such as steaks and chops. Offal can also be grilled.

Trimming fat from steak

Trim all but a very thin rim of fat from the meat and on steaks, slash the rest at 2.5 cm (1 inch) intervals to prevent the meat from curling. Before grilling, all meat should be lightly brushed with oil to prevent sticking. The oil can be flavoured with wine or cider, chopped herbs or spices such as paprika, cumin and coriander. Season with pepper but not salt as this draws out the juices.

If you have time, marinate the meat in a flavoured mixture to improve taste and tenderness.

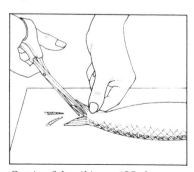

Cutting fish tail into a 'V' shape

FISH

You can grill whole small fish or fish fillets. Small fish should be properly cleaned with fins removed. The heads can be left on if wished and the tails should be trimmed in a neat V-shape.

Fish also benefits from being brushed with oil and seasoned.

VEGETABLES

Types which can be grilled include mushrooms, courgettes,

Grilling vegetables

aubergines, peppers and tomatoes. Brush them with a flavoured oil and either lay the vegetables directly on the grill rack or put on to kebab skewers.

METHOD

If you have an open, wire grill rack under a conventional grill, first cover it with perforated foil. Turn the grill to high and get the foil hot.

For meat, lay it on the hot rack. Grill one side until done, turn over and cook the other side. Lamb and beef can be rare, medium or well done. Pork must be well done.

For whole fish, cook the same as for meat. Fillets of oily fish should be laid, cut side up, on the grill and cooked only on that side. White fish fillets are best placed in a shallow, heatproof dish. Cutlets can be cooked like whole fish.

Instead of serving grilled foods with the usual savoury butters, make yogurt sauces by beating natural yogurt with herbs, spices, lemon juice and tomato purée etc.

DRY-FRYING

Dry-frying, or pan grilling, is particularly suited to all types of good quality meats.

If possible, use a ridged cast-iron pan or broiler. This enables much of the fat to drain from the meat, besides giving it an attractive ridged pattern.

METHOD

Prepare the meat as for grilling. Lightly oil the pan and place on a high heat until the oil sizzles. Lay

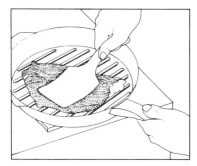

Dry-frying meat

the meat in the hot pan and cook for 1 minute, pressing down against the ridges. Turn and cook the second side in the same way. Lower the heat to medium. If possible, turn the meat at right angles to its original position. Cook for the remaining time on that side. Turn again and complete cooking.

As with conventionally grilled meats, garnish with flavoured yogurt.

STIR-FRYING

Stir-frying, a method of cooking taken from the Chinese, can be used for meat, fish, vegetables or nuts. The cooking process is extremely quick, which preserves vitamins and also prevents the ingredients from soaking up too much oil.

All ingredients for stir-frying must be cut into small, thin slices before cooking begins.

Use a lightly flavoured oil such as groundnut, sunflower or safflower. Choose flavourers such

as garlic and ground ginger. Try small amounts of liquid such as sherry or soy sauce for adding at the end if wished.

You will need a large, heavy frying pan or a wok. Those with electric cookers may well find a flat based wok more effective than one that is round based. A wooden or perforated spoon or fish-slice is necessary for moving the ingredients around.

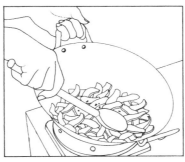

Stir-frying thinly sliced food

METHOD

Heat the oil in the wok on a high heat. Add those ingredients that need a longer cooking time, plus the dry flavourers. Stir-fry for about 2 minutes. Add other ingredients and continue to stir until all are done (the process is rarely longer than about 6 minutes and the vegetables should still be crisp). Add liquid ingredients if using and serve as soon as possible.

STEAMING

Steaming is a light method of cooking which involves no fats and

A large steamer for fatless cooking

preserves both nutrients and flavour. It is particularly suited to vegetables and fish. Chicken also steams effectively.

A large steamer is a useful piece of equipment in any kitchen. It consists of a saucepan with a perforated container that sits inside it and a well-fitting lid.

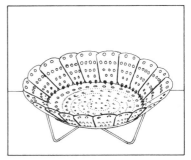

Small steamers fit into saucepans

You can also buy small steamers which open up rather like a flower and can be fitted into any sized saucepan. Failing this, use a steamproof colander that can sit neatly in a saucepan and be covered with foil.

VEGETABLES

Cut them into fairly small, even sized pieces. If mixing vegetables, make sure that they have similar cooking times.

METHOD

Put the prepared vegetables into the steamer. Bring the water to the boil in the saucepan. Lower in the steamer. The water must not bubble up and touch the vegetables. If there is too much water, pour some away. Cover the pan and cook until the vegetables are just tender. They will take about half as long again as boiled vegetables, and when done should still be slightly crisp. Serve as soon as possible.

FISH

Use white fish fillets, cut into portions, fish cutlets, small whole fish such as whiting, or thin flat-fish fillets which should be rolled or folded. Season well with pepper, spices and herbs.

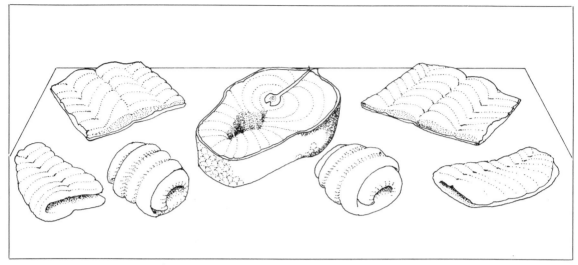

Fish responds well to steaming. Season well with spices and herbs first

Fish must always be steamed in a closed container in order to keep flavour and juices. Large enamel plates which fit inside the steamer are ideal since they conduct heat efficiently. Foil can also be used.

METHOD
Lightly grease the plates or foil. Put the fish on one plate and cover

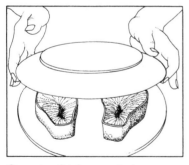

Steaming fish between 2 plates

with the other. Or line the steamer with foil. Put on the fish. Cover completely with the sides of the foil. Fish portions can also be individually wrapped in foil parcels.

Bring a saucepan of water to the boil. Lay the plates on top or lower in the steamer. The water must not touch the container. Steam until the fish is done. Steamed fish cooks extremely

quickly—thin fillets need about 8 minutes, thick cutlets about 20 minutes.

CHICKEN
Flavour joints with ingredients such as soy or Worcestershire sauce. Wrap in parcels of oiled foil. Place in the steamer for about 45 minutes.

BOILING AND POACHING
Both meat and fish can be simmered gently in a flavoured liquid until they are tender, moist and full of flavour. With meat, the process is usually called boiling. When a similar method is used for fish, it is called poaching.

MEAT AND POULTRY
Lean beef joints, lean pork, leg or rolled breast of lamb and whole

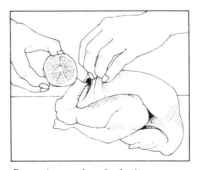

Preparing poultry for boiling

chickens can all be boiled. Bacon joints and salt beef are also suitable.

Salt meats should be soaked for 8 hours in cold water and drained. All meats should be securely tied. Chickens can be rubbed with spices such as paprika or curry spices and bunches of herbs, or a half lemon can be put inside the body cavity.

METHOD
Put the meat or poultry into a large saucepan and add enough water to just cover meat joints and to come just over the legs of the chicken. Add a large onion, carrot and celery stick, a bouquet garni and 5 ml (1 tsp) black peppercorns, plus 5 ml (1 tsp) whole cloves for salt meats. A little cider, wine or beer can also be added if wished. Bring the liquid to just below boiling point. Cover and simmer gently until tender. Meats need about 25 minutes per 450 g (1 lb), chicken 20 minutes.

Vegetables can be cooked with boiled meats. Add them towards the end of the cooking time, so that when the meat is tender the vegetables are cooked too. Suitable vegetables include carrots, celery, wedges of firm cabbage, whole small onions, and broad beans and peas tied loosely in muslin bags.

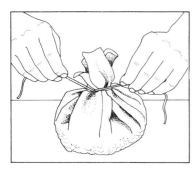
Tie beans in muslin for boiling

Boiled meat and poultry can be served hot or cold. The stock produced when boiling unsalted meats may be used as a thin gravy or can be made into a sauce by stirring 300 ml ($\frac{1}{2}$ pint) into 15 g ($\frac{1}{2}$ oz) melted margarine or butter and 15 ml (1 tbsp) wholewheat flour. Chopped herbs and pickles, such as capers or gherkins, can be added for flavour. The stock from salted meats is too salty to make a pleasant sauce. Salted meats are best served plainly with their vegetable accompaniments.

If the meat is to be served cold, cool it in the stock to room temperature and, if possible, leave in a cool place for at least 2 hours after removing from the stock.

Pickles are a favourite accompaniment for boiled meats. They can also be diced and mixed into salads, with flavoured oil and vinegar or yogurt based dressings.

FISH
Fish is poached in a flavoured liquid often known as a court bouillon.

Use absolutely fresh fish as the method brings out the natural flavour. Use whole small or large fish, both round or flat, thick fish fillets or cutlets, and smoked fish such as kippers and smoked cod or haddock fillets.

METHOD
Use a large pan, big enough to take the fish without bending (an oval one is ideal). It is a good idea to put a trivet or small rack in the base of the pan. If you use a purpose-made fish kettle, it will have a built-in plate. Place a piece of muslin under both this and the fish so that the fish can be lifted out easily. A clean linen tea towel or foil can also be used.

For fresh fish, put a glass of dry white wine into the pan and enough water to just cover the fish. Add 5 ml (1 tsp) black peppercorns, a bouquet garni and an onion, carrot and celery stick, roughly chopped. A blade of mace will give an additional pleasant flavour.

Smoked fish can be poached in plain water with the same flavourings or in a mixture of half water and half milk.

For water based mixtures, bring them to the boil, cover and simmer for 10 minutes. Cool to just below simmering and carefully lower in the fish. Cook until the flesh flakes easily when tested with a fork.

Small fillets take about 5 minutes, smoked about 5 minutes, fillets 6–10 minutes depending on thickness, whole fish from 15–30 minutes depending on size.

Milk based liquids should be infused with the flavourings on a low heat for 5 minutes before the fish is added and cooked as before.

BRAISING
When meat is braised, it is generally first browned in butter or oil, after which vegetables are softened in the same fat. This gives an added richness to the final flavour. This effect can be achieved without fat.

METHOD
Put 150 ml ($\frac{1}{4}$ pint) stock into a flameproof casserole, bring to the boil and add the braising vegetables (usually chopped onion, carrot and/or celery). Cook over a medium heat until beginning to soften and the stock has reduced to about 45 ml (3 tbsp). Raise the heat, put in the meat and sear it on all sides. Add any remaining stock or flavouring ingredients, cover and cook in the oven for the required amount of time.

COLD START CASSEROLES
Many casseroles can be successfully made without involving the initial searing process.

METHOD
Dice lean meat and any vegetable ingredients. Layer these in a flameproof casserole with seasonings and other dry flavouring ingredients (herbs, spices). Pour in enough liquid to just cover. This can be water or stock or a mixture. Up to 150 ml ($\frac{1}{4}$ pint) can be replaced by wine or cider, up to 300 ml ($\frac{1}{2}$ pint) by beer. Add other flavourings such as tomato purée or Worcestershire sauce.

Place the casserole on top of the cooker over a moderate heat. Bring the liquid to the boil. Cover and cook in the oven for the required amount of time.

SAUTÉ DISHES
Sauté dishes also usually involve an initial frying process. As with braising, there is an alternative.

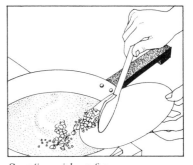
Sautéing without fat

METHOD
Bring 150 ml ($\frac{1}{4}$ pint) stock to the boil in a deep frying pan or sauté pan. Put in one chopped onion and a chopped garlic clove. Boil until the liquid is reduced to about 30 ml (2 tbsp). Put in the meat and sear it.

Stir in wholewheat flour to thicken if necessary. Stir in stock or a mixture of wine or stock. Add herbs if using. Cover and cook gently for the required amount of time.

Basic Recipes

In this chapter you will find a wide selection of deliciously healthy recipes, which serve as a useful basic repertoire. There's yogurt to make at home, sauces, dressings and spreads, traditional and exotic breads, pastry, pasta and pizza.

YOGURT

It is not necessary to invest in a commercial yogurt machine; a wide-necked insulated jar and a thermometer are the only essential equipment. Use either skimmed or semi-skimmed milk, skimmed milk powder, raw, pasteurised milk, sterilised or UHT. (UHT is already sterilised so it is the most convenient to use and results in a richer texture. It does not have to be boiled; just heated to the correct temperature.) Condensed and evaporated milks do not always give such good results. You can buy special yogurt starter cultures, but it is simpler at first to use bought natural yogurt. For your next batch, keep back a little

Flavouring natural yogurt

from the first yogurt you made. You can do this about three times, then buy a new starter tub of natural yogurt. To obtain a thick, creamy yogurt, add skimmed milk powder (see recipe). Flavour the finished yogurt with fruit or honey, if liked.

NATURAL YOGURT

Makes about 600 ml (1 pint)

568 ml (1 pint) milk

25 ml (1½ tbsp) natural yogurt

30 ml (2 tbsp) skimmed milk powder (optional)

1 Use absolutely clean, well rinsed containers and utensils. Warm an insulated jar. Pour the milk into a saucepan and bring to the boil. (If you want a thick

yogurt, keep the pan on a very low heat after this for 15 minutes.) Remove from the heat and allow to cool to 45°C (113°F). (If you are using UHT or sterilised milk, bring them up to 45°C (113°F).)

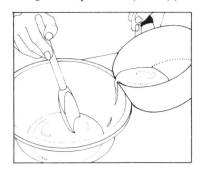

2 Spoon the natural yogurt into a bowl and stir in a little of the cooled milk. Add the skimmed milk powder, if used, to make a smooth paste. Stir in the remaining milk.

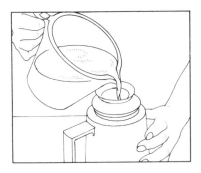

3 Pour into the warmed insulated jar. Cover and leave for 8–9 hours, undisturbed.

4 Transfer the yogurt into small pots or cartons and place in the refrigerator immediately. It will keep for up to 10 days.

SAUCES, DRESSINGS AND SPREADS

A good sauce or dressing can transform everyday food into something special, but they are all too often fattening and unhealthy! These recipes have been specially chosen to include in a healthy diet to add interest and flavour without being too calorie-laden.

BLENDER TOMATO DRESSING

Makes about 150 ml ($\frac{1}{4}$ pint)

30 ml (2 tbsp) tomato juice

30 ml (2 tbsp) cider vinegar

30 ml (2 tbsp) clear honey

1 egg yolk

salt and freshly ground pepper

30 ml (2 tbsp) chopped fresh chives

sprig of parsley

60 ml (4 tbsp) sunflower oil

1 Put the tomato juice, vinegar, honey, egg yolk, seasoning, chives and parsley in a blender or food processor and blend for 30 seconds.

2 Gradually add the sunflower oil and blend until smooth. Use as a dressing for crisp mixed vegetable salads.

SOURED CREAM AND WATERCRESS DRESSING

This dressing is better made at least 30 minutes before serving.

Serves 4

$\frac{1}{2}$ bunch of watercress

150 ml ($\frac{1}{4}$ pint) soured cream

2.5 ml ($\frac{1}{2}$ tsp) lemon juice

salt and freshly ground pepper

a little milk

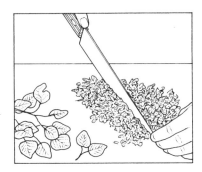

1 Remove and discard the coarse stalks, then chop the watercress finely.

2 Mix with the soured cream and lemon juice and season to taste.

3 Add enough milk to give a pouring consistency.

4 Good with bean and pulse salads. Also goes well with cold fish dishes and baked potatoes.

YOGURT DRESSING

Makes 150 ml ($\frac{1}{4}$ pint)

150 ml ($\frac{1}{4}$ pint) natural yogurt

1.25 ml ($\frac{1}{4}$ tsp) mustard powder

salt and freshly ground pepper

15 ml (1 tbsp) lemon juice

15 ml (1 tbsp) chopped fresh parsley

1 Place the yogurt, mustard, seasoning, lemon juice and parsley in a bowl.

2 Mix well together. Serve with crunchy vegetable salads such as shredded cabbage, cauliflower and Chinese leaves.

YOGURT AND MUSTARD SAUCE

Makes 225 ml (8 fl oz)

225 ml (8 fl oz) natural yogurt

15 ml (1 tbsp) finely chopped onion

15 ml (1 tbsp) made mustard

1.25 ml ($\frac{1}{4}$ level tsp) salt

freshly ground pepper

15 ml (1 tbsp) chopped fresh parsley or finely chopped chives, to garnish

1 Stir together the yogurt with the onion, mustard and seasoning in a saucepan over a gentle heat. Do not allow the mixture to boil.

2 Garnish with the chopped parsley or chives before serving.

3 Good with raw spinach and as a topping for baked potatoes. Also good with oily fish or beef.

WATERCRESS SAUCE

Makes 225 ml (8 fl oz)

25 g (1 oz) margarine or butter

1 onion, skinned and thinly sliced

1 small garlic clove, skinned

2 bunches of watercress, trimmed and chopped

60 ml (4 tbsp) white wine

30 ml (2 tbsp) stock

5 ml (1 tsp) Barbados sugar

1 Melt the margarine in a small saucepan and gently fry the onion and garlic for about 10 minutes or until the onion is tender but not browned. Discard the garlic.

2 Add the watercress to the onion. Stir in the wine, stock and sugar and cook the mixture for about 3 minutes until the watercress is tender.

3 Purée the mixture in a blender or food processor or rub through a sieve to make a smooth sauce. Heat through gently. Serve with baked or steamed fish.

SHARP GOOSEBERRY SAUCE

Makes 300 ml ($\frac{1}{2}$ pint)

225 g (8 oz) gooseberries, topped
   and tailed

25 g (1 oz) margarine or butter

30–60 ml (2–4 tbsp) Barbados sugar

1 Wash and stew the fruit in a
saucepan with as little water as
possible, until soft and pulped,
stirring occasionally. Purée the
mixture in a blender or food
processor or rub through a sieve
until smooth.

2 Stir in the margarine and
sugar to taste and heat
through. Serve hot with baked or
grilled mackerel.

WHOLEMEAL BREAD SAUCE

Makes about 300 ml ($\frac{1}{2}$ pint)

3 cloves

1 small onion, skinned

300 ml ($\frac{1}{2}$ pint) milk

$\frac{1}{2}$ bay leaf

1 blade of mace

50 g (2 oz) wholemeal breadcrumbs

salt and freshly ground pepper

15 g ($\frac{1}{2}$ oz) margarine or butter
   (optional)

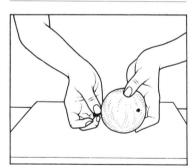

1 Push the cloves into the onion.
Put the milk into a saucepan
with the onion, bay leaf and mace.

2 Bring gently to the boil,
remove from the heat and
leave to stand for 15 minutes.

3 Strain the milk and return to
the pan with the breadcrumbs.
Season the mixture and heat
gently, stirring, until boiling.

4 Beat in the margarine, if using,
and serve the sauce hot as an
accompaniment to poultry.

VEGETABLE DISHES

Vegetables play an important part
in a healthy diet. Raw vegetables
are particularly good, losing none
of their goodness in the cooking
process. But if you want to ring
the changes with cooked vegetables, try these recipes for a tasty
alternative to the usual method of
plain boiling.

UNPEELED ROAST POTATOES

Serves 4

900 g (2 lb) small or medium old
   potatoes

50 g (2 oz) margarine or butter,
   or 30 ml (2 tbsp) vegetable oil

1 Scrub the potatoes and cut
them into 2.5 cm (1 inch)
cubes.

2 Place the margarine in a large
shallow roasting tin and put in
the oven at 220°C (425°F) mark 7
until the fat is melted and hot.

3 Mix the potatoes into the
margarine and bake in the
oven for 1 hour, stirring occasionally, until really crisp and golden
brown.

CAULIFLOWER NIÇOISE

Serves 4

1 cauliflower

salt

15 ml (1 tbsp) vegetable oil

1 small onion, skinned and
   chopped

1–2 garlic cloves, skinned and
   crushed

3 tomatoes, skinned and quartered

finely grated rind and juice of 1
   lemon

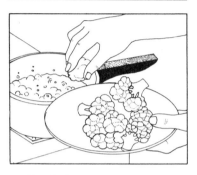

1 Break the cauliflower into
florets, place in a saucepan of
boiling salted water and cook for 5
minutes. Drain and place in a
warmed serving dish. Keep hot.

2 Heat the oil in a pan, add the
onion and garlic and fry for 3
minutes. Add the tomatoes and
cook for 3 minutes. Add the lemon
juice and cook for a further 2
minutes.

3 Pour over the cauliflower and
serve sprinkled with finely
grated lemon rind.

STEAMED MANGE-TOUT

Serves 6

700 g (1½ lb) mange-tout
salt and freshly ground pepper

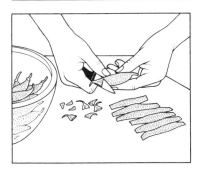

1 Top and tail the pods and remove any side strings. Place in
a colander or steamer over a pan of
boiling, salted water (see page 149).

2 Cover and steam gently for
about 5 minutes or until just
tender. Do not overcook. Spoon
into a warmed serving dish, toss
gently with seasoning.

DHAL (LENTIL PURÉE)

Serves 4

100 g (4 oz) red lentils
300 ml (½ pint) cold water
30 ml (2 tbsp) sunflower oil
1 medium onion, skinned and
finely chopped
25 g (1 oz) margarine or butter
salt and freshly ground pepper

1 Rinse the lentils and put in a
saucepan with the cold water.
Bring to the boil and simmer for
about 1 hour until tender, adding
more water if they get too dry.

2 Meanwhile, heat the oil in a
pan, add the onion and fry for
5 minutes until soft.

3 When the lentils are tender,
remove from the heat and stir
vigorously to form a purée. Add
the margarine and fried onion and
stir over the heat. Season.

BREADS

Bread-making need not be limited
to the usual yeasted loaf alone.
You can try your hand at making
your own more exotic breads such
as puris, chappattis and parathas
from India, and pitta, the popular
Greek bread, all made with
wholemeal flour for extra flavour
and goodness.

WHOLEMEAL BREAD

*Makes two 900 g (2 lb) or four 450 g
(1 lb) loaves*

50 g (2 oz) fresh yeast or 30 ml
(2 tbsp) dried and 5 ml (1 tsp)
honey
900 ml (1½ pints) tepid water
1.4 kg (3 lb) plain wholemeal flour
30 ml (2 tbsp) demerara sugar
20 ml (4 tsp) salt
25 g (1 oz) margarine or butter
cracked wheat

1 Grease two 900 g (2 lb) or four
450 g (1 lb) loaf tins. Blend the
fresh yeast with 300 ml (½ pint) of
the water. If using dried yeast,
dissolve the honey in 300 ml
(½ pint) of the water and sprinkle
over the yeast. Leave the fresh or
dried yeast liquid in a warm place
for 15 minutes until frothy.

2 Mix the flour, sugar and salt
together in a large bowl. Rub
in the margarine. Stir in the yeast
liquid, adding enough of the
remaining water to make a firm
dough that leaves the bowl clean.

3 Turn out on to a lightly
floured surface and knead the
dough until firm, elastic and no
longer sticky. Shape into a ball,
cover with a clean cloth and leave
to rise in a warm place for about 1
hour until doubled in size.

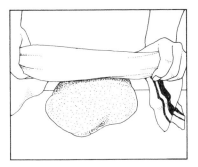

4 Turn the dough on to a
floured surface and knead
again until firm. Divide into 2 or
4 pieces and flatten firmly with
the knuckles to knock out any air
bubbles. Knead well until firm.

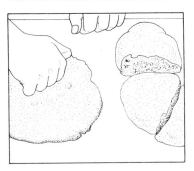

5 Shape the dough into the tins.
Brush with salted water and
sprinkle with cracked wheat.
Cover with a cloth and leave to
prove for 1 hour at room
temperature until the dough rises
to the tops of the tins.

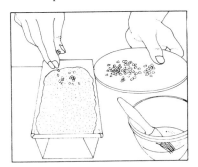

6 Bake in the oven at 230°C
(450°F) mark 8 for 30–40
minutes until well risen and firm.
Cool on a wire rack.

CHAPPATTIS

Makes about 6

100 g (4 oz) plain wholemeal flour

1.25 ml ($\frac{1}{4}$ tsp) salt

5 ml (1 tsp) baking powder

15 g ($\frac{1}{2}$ oz) margarine or butter

90 ml (6 tbsp) water

vegetable oil for frying

1 Mix together the flour, salt and baking powder in a bowl. Rub in the margarine and add enough water to mix to a stiff dough. Turn on to a floured surface and knead well for 10 minutes.

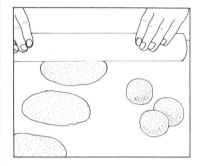

2 Divide the dough into 6–8 pieces and shape each into a small ball. Roll each ball into a 10 cm (4 inch) round.

3 Heat the oil in a frying pan and fry the chappattis one at a time until they puff up, turning once. Drain on absorbent kitchen paper and serve while still warm as an accompaniment to a curry.

PARATHAS

Makes 12

350 g (12 oz) plain wholemeal flour

5 ml (1 tsp) salt

300 ml ($\frac{1}{2}$ pint) water

100 g (4 oz) ghee or clarified butter, melted

1 Mix the flour and salt together in a bowl. Add the water and bind to a soft pliable dough — it may be slightly sticky. Knead lightly, using a little flour if necessary. Cover and leave to rest for about 15 minutes.

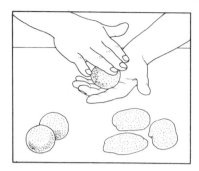

2 Divide the dough into 12 and roll each piece into a smooth ball using the palms of your hands.

3 On a lightly floured surface, roll each ball out into a 15 cm (6 inch) round.

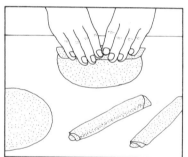

4 Smear a little cooled but not set ghee over each one and roll up like cigars.

5 Lift up the roll and place one end in the centre of your hand. Carefully wind the rest of the roll around the centre point to form a disc. Press lightly together.

6 Roll out each round on a floured surface to a 12.5–5 cm (5–6 inch) circle.

7 Heat a frying pan. When really hot, cook a paratha until bubbles appear. Flip over.

8 Cook the underside for about 30 seconds while smearing the top with ghee.

9 Turn over the paratha twice more, smearing the second side with ghee. When browned, remove from pan. Wipe pan between frying parathas.

PITTA BREAD

Makes 8

15 g ($\frac{1}{2}$ oz) fresh yeast or 7.5 ml (1$\frac{1}{2}$ tsp) dried and 5 ml (1 tsp) Barbados sugar

about 300 ml ($\frac{1}{2}$ pint) tepid water

450 g (1 lb) strong wholemeal flour

2.5 ml ($\frac{1}{2}$ tsp) salt

1 Grease a baking sheet. Blend the yeast with a little of the water. If using dried yeast, dissolve the sugar in the water and sprinkle over the yeast. Leave the fresh or dried yeast in a warm place for 15 minutes until frothy.

2 Sift the flour and salt into a bowl and make a well in the centre. Add the yeast liquid and remaining water. Mix to a dough.

3 Turn out on to a floured surface and knead for about 10 minutes. Place in a bowl, cover with lightly oiled polythene and leave to rise in a warm place for 2 hours until doubled in size.

4 Knead on a floured surface for 2–3 minutes. Divide the dough into 8 even pieces, knead each into a ball and flatten to about 0.5 cm ($\frac{1}{4}$ inch) thick.

5 Place on the baking sheet, cover with lightly oiled polythene and leave to prove in a warm place until doubled in size.

6 Bake in the oven at 230°C (450°F) mark 8 for about 10 minutes. Cool on a wire rack.

PURIS
(INDIAN WAFERS)

Makes 8

100 g (4 oz) plain wholemeal flour
15 g ($\frac{1}{2}$ oz) margarine or butter
salt and freshly ground pepper
about 60 ml (4 tbsp) water
sunflower oil, for frying

1 Put the flour in a bowl and rub in the margarine. Season. Gradually work in just enough water to give a pliable dough and knead well. If time permits, cover and leave the dough for 1 hour.

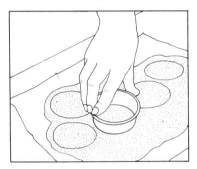

2 Roll out the dough wafer-thin between sheets of non-stick paper, then cut out rounds about 7.5 cm (3 inches) in diameter. If they are not to be fried at once, cover the rounds with a damp cloth.

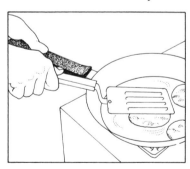

3 Heat the oil in a frying pan and fry the rounds one or two at a time: slide each raw puri into the oil and hold it down with a slotted spatula, pressing lightly to distribute the air.

4 Turn once, then drain on absorbent kitchen paper. Serve as an accompaniment to a curry.

PASTRY, PASTA AND PIZZA

There is no need to rule out pastries, pastas and pizzas when following a healthy eating plan. They are more nutritious when made with wholemeal flour rather than white, and a fresh pizza or bowl of pasta need not be laden with calories as long as you choose toppings and fillings carefully.

WHOLEMEAL PASTRY

For wholemeal pastry the proportion of flour to fat is two to one. Therefore, for a recipe requiring 250 g (8 oz) pastry, make up the pastry using 250 g (8 oz) flour and 125 g (4 oz) fat.

When a recipe requires 175 g (6 oz) pastry, this refers to the weight of flour.

Makes 175 g (6 oz)

175 g (6 oz) plain wholemeal flour
pinch of salt
75 g (3 oz) margarine or butter

1 Mix the flour and salt together in a bowl and add the margarine in small pieces. Using both hands, rub the margarine into the flour between finger and thumb tips until there are no lumps of margarine left and the mixture resembles fine breadcrumbs.

2 Add 30 ml (2 tbsp) water all at once, sprinkling it evenly over the surface.

3 Stir the water in with a round-bladed knife until the mixture begins to stick together in large lumps.

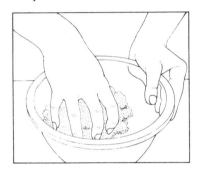

4 With one hand, collect the mixture together and knead lightly for a few seconds, to give a firm smooth dough. The pastry can be used straight away, but is better allowed to 'rest' for 15 minutes. It can also be wrapped in polythene and kept in the refrigerator for 1–2 days.

5 When the pastry is required, sprinkle a very little flour on the working surface and on the rolling pin, not on the pastry, and roll out the dough evenly in one direction only, turning occasionally. The usual thickness is about 0.3 cm ($\frac{1}{8}$ inch). Do not pull or stretch the dough. Use as required. The usual oven temperature for wholemeal pastry is 200–220°C (400–425°F) mark 6–7.

WHOLEMEAL PASTA

Wholemeal noodles will keep for 2–3 days if covered and stored in the refrigerator.

Makes about 350 g (12 oz)

175 g (6 oz) plain wholemeal flour

1 egg

1 egg white

30 ml (2 tbsp) olive oil

5 ml (1 tsp) salt

1 Place the flour in a large bowl. Make a well in the centre and add the egg, egg white, oil, salt and 15 ml (1 tbsp) water. Mix together to form a soft dough.

2 Knead the dough for 10 minutes on a lightly floured surface until smooth and elastic. Re-flour the surface and roll out the dough to form a large paper-thin rectangle of pasta.

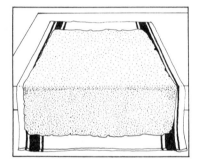

3 Lay the pasta on a clean dry cloth. Let one third of the pasta sheet hang over the side of the table and turn it every 10 minutes. This will help to dry the pasta more quickly.

4 The drying process takes about 30 minutes and the pasta is ready to cut when it is dry and looks leathery.

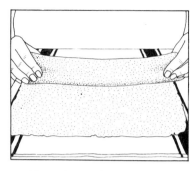

5 To make noodles, roll the pasta up loosely into a roll about 7.5 cm (3 inches) wide.

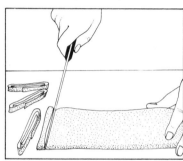

6 Cut the roll into 0.5 cm (¼ inch) slices and leave for 10 minutes.

7 To serve, cook in boiling salted water for about 8 minutes until just tender.

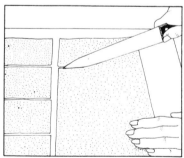

8 To make lasagne, cut the pasta dough into the desired size of rectangles. Leave on a floured tea towel for 10 minutes before using.

Serving suggestions

Toss hot drained noodles in a little margarine or butter, then sprinkle with black pepper, herbs, ham and grated cheese.

WHOLEMEAL PIZZA DOUGH

Serves 4

15 g (½ oz) fresh yeast or 10 ml (2 tsp) dried and 2.5 ml (½ tsp) Barbados sugar

150 ml (¼ pint) tepid milk

225 g (8 oz) plain wholemeal flour

pinch of salt

50 g (2 oz) margarine or butter

1 egg, beaten

1 Blend the fresh yeast into the milk. If using dried yeast, dissolve the sugar in the milk and sprinkle over the yeast. Leave the fresh or dried yeast in a warm place for 15 minutes until frothy.

2 Mix the flour and salt together in a bowl. Rub in the margarine, then stir in the yeast mixture and egg.

3 Knead on a floured surface for 10 minutes. Place in the bowl, cover with a tea towel and rise in a warm place for 1 hour until doubled in size.

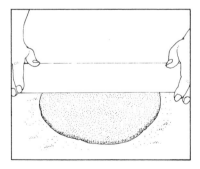

4 Knead the dough and roll out to a 23 cm (9 inch) round. Use as required.

INDEX